LOVE, LONELINESS, ABUSE, AND MURDER

THE **TRUE STORY** OF A WOMAN
DESPERATELY SEEKING COMPANIONSHIP

Jim B. Pulley

MILL CITY PRESS, INC.

212 3RD AVENUE NORTH, SUITE 290

MINNEAPOLIS, MN 55401

612.455.2294

WWW.MILLCITYPUBLISHING.COM

ISBN-13: 978-1-937600-12-9

LCCN: 2011938216

TYPESET BY WENDY BAKER

PRINTED IN THE UNITED STATES OF AMERICA

LOVE, LONELINESS, ABUSE, AND MURDER

Table of Contents

Jim B. Pulley

Preface

INSPIRATION FOR WRITING THIS TRUE account of my mother's murder came from several places. Originally I had placed the responsibility squarely on my own shoulders. Like most people, I had taken the attitude of, "I'll get 'round-to-it." This wasn't the least bit helpful.

In January of 2009 two people came into my office on an insurance appointment. Our time was spent discussing the man's life insurance. Having never met this couple I really had no way of knowing what kind of impact they could possibly have on my life. Ron had terminal cancer. Darese, his wife, was desperate for advice. Once we had the paperwork on Ron's life insurance sorted out, it wasn't five weeks before he passed away.

This was the beginning of a working relationship between me and Darese Cotton. As fate would have it, she is a writer. Her teaching background along with her life's experiences led her to begin penning a novel. When I learned this, I told her that I had a story to tell.

Darese has been a huge part of the reason that I wrote this book. She has been nothing but supportive and positive in her role as my editor and mentor, and I thank her for it.

I also have to thank my wife, Sheri, for putting up with my disrupting fourteen months of our daily routine to forge my way through the process of completing this book.

My thoughts and prayers go out to the investigators and detectives with the City of Duncanville Police Department. My entire family will forever hold all of the individuals involved in high regard. Gloria Backus got the ball rolling with her diligent work in providing me with the case files. The Freedom of Information Act made it possible for me to obtain the files. The difficult task of reading the actual reports brought quite a bit of stress into my life. They supplied me with all the facts that my memory may have erased. When recording the officers' reports, I kept them as accurate as possible.

The decision to include my mom's personal writing was mine. I felt that since the words were in her handwriting, they had been written for a reason. This book was created from fact. My only hope is that one of you out there will gain positive motivation to improve your own personal situation after reading my mom's story.

Chapter One

Going Through the Motions

S IGNS OF SPRING WERE EVERYWHERE on that warm April day when I walked into my mother's house. The scene didn't seem real since the place was completely empty. Immediately my nostrils were filled with an unfamiliar odor. The house had been closed up for a few weeks. My uncle Bob and I were there to take care of removing a piece of carpet that had been ruined by a blood stain. The spot was where my mom had fallen after being shot one time in the face.

Her husband (not my dad) had pulled a .22-caliber handgun on her. He didn't hesitate to use it. The pistol was the type that forces the user to pull the hammer back before pulling the trigger. *Single shot* is the term; you know, just a little Saturday night special. Not so special when he fired a shot that hit her just below the right eye. The coroner told us the slug passed through her cranium and cracked her skull in the back. This thoughtless act killed her instantly.

Mom had just seen us four weeks earlier on her sixtieth birthday. We laughed and joked so much during her visit that we were all crying. Pictures from that weekend show her letting loose and enjoying her family like old times. Life can surely change in an instant.

Entering the master bedroom, Bob offered to carry out the task alone. I put aside all the emotions that were whisking through me at ninety miles an hour. Bob had done two or three tours in Vietnam so I assumed a little blood didn't upset him. One of our friends had placed a nightstand over the large blood-soaked area. It was a hurried attempt to protect me and everyone else while we were cleaning out the house after Mom's funeral. When we moved the table, a chilling emptiness came over me. Everything I knew and understood had been completely ripped from our lives. Bob pulled out a razor-sharp knife. With a few well-placed cuts our business was complete. We neatly rolled up the carpet. Hoisting the rug to our shoulders, we carried it out to the dumpster. That's how we started the morning.

I had arranged a meeting with the insurance claims adjuster that same day. Bob left to go to work. The word "alone" suddenly had a very clear meaning. Black powder from the crime scene unit was all over the woodwork, window sills, and doorways. The black smears were anywhere the investigators felt they could lift a fingerprint.

Where do I start to explain how being in my own mother's house could chill me so deeply? The person we felt certain was responsible for her killing was out of jail on bail. I had no idea if he was stalking around the empty house waiting on me or my brother to show up. I knew full well what he was capable of.

At one point I stood with my back against the wall, my heart beating so hard I could feel each pulse in my eyes. My breathing had increased. Mentally, I allowed every pop and crack of the house to become something it wasn't. Like a rattled ten-year-old, I had left the front door open. This wasn't a scene from a Hitchcock thriller; it was the sad reality of our lives at that time. Anger, fear, frustration, even exhaustion controlled my thoughts and actions.

The minutes seemed to drag as I waited for the insurance adjuster. Thoughts of what had happened only a few short weeks before raced through my mind. Giving in to my feelings, I wound up waiting in my car until the claims rep showed up.

Upon the adjuster's arrival we entered the house together. As we moved from the entry way, we stepped down into the large living area. To the right was the hallway; the dining room was directly to our left. From our visits, I knew the layout of Mom's house well. The insurance representative had his clipboard ready. I am not sure if he was truly prepared for the overall scene. There was leftover fingerprint powder in every conceivable spot where a person could have placed his or her hands. The door frame leading to the bedrooms was covered in the gray substance. Passing the guest bathroom, I couldn't help but notice the broken door. The strike plate, which should have been mounted in the stained wood trim, was lying on the marble countertop. The door had a fist indentation. The splintered wooden frame was a telltale sign of the horror that went on inside of Mom's own home.

At the end of the hallway, we walked into the master bedroom. I explained why the carpet was missing. There was no need to mention the three-foot blood stain on the exposed concrete floor. The light of the morning reflected from the pool through the sliding glass door. There we stood, business at hand, just a few steps from where my mother had fallen. The house was as empty as I felt inside.

Mom's master bath was just off her bedroom. The door had been damaged beyond use. More punch marks showing the anger and hatred that came from within her disturbed so-called husband.

Moving down the hall, we turned back into the sunken living room. The design was unique. The house had been built with the great room in the center. There were actually six interior walls, giving the room a special flavor. Stepping up to the kitchen on our final pass, we could see where the screen on the other sliding door had been torn. In one of his many drunken moments, Mom's husband had literally walked right through the screening. She would just take a deep sigh and shake her head when she would tell us of similar escapades.

The front of Mom's house had a big wooden double door. On the left side was a thick panel which was strictly for show. I pulled the heavy dark oak door closed behind us. We silently walked to his van. Inside he completed my claim. Using a portable printer, a check popped out. The amount was adequate to start the long process of cleaning up the crime scene.

All the while, I was forcing myself through the agony. No one else was responsible for this property. I focused on cleaning up, and repairing Mom's house. This became one way of deflecting my feelings. I would tuck them away and aim my sights on a goal that seemed to distract me from the life-altering trauma of Mom's murder.

Patricia Lou Montgomery was born in 1935 on Saint Patrick's Day. Her father was a tenant farmer who taught himself masonry. This learning experience came along when he agreed to build a water well for a few extra dollars. Her mother was a God-fearing woman and mother to six children. Grandma never had a harsh word to say about anyone. Mom grew up understanding hard work. She had daily duties, like feeding the chickens, along with other typical farm chores. Their entertainment came in the way of baseball games with the neighbors or dressing up their youngest sister, Carolyn.

Mom was educated in a one-room school. Each grade was separated by the row of desks in which you were seated. She was a pretty sharp girl. They moved her from the second to the fourth, making her young for her grade. I guess that move created the opportunity for my dad, Jack, and her to meet. Van Buren High in Indiana is the place. Just outside of Marion off State Road Eighteen. Uncle Bud Martz had a grocery store there for many years. As you walked into the grocery, the worn wooden floors slanted to the right. There were distinct odors of fresh potatoes and ground beef. In my mind's eye, I can see Uncle Bud wearing an apron bloodied from cutting meat for his customers. Those days, like so many, are far removed, but the memories are always pleasant.

Jack C. Pulley was shipped off to Korea not long after the two were married. Mom's loving husband stood taller than his five feet nine inches showed. The handsome young man with dark wavy hair was stronger than his physical appearance. He stood proud as a member

of the army's Third Infantry Division. Dad was promoted in the field to sergeant. I feel this was an early indication of his natural leadership skills. Jack C. Pulley always kept a great sense of humor about him. Nothing was ever said about what all went on during his time on the front lines. You can bet that Dad kept them all laughing despite their unspeakable circumstances.

Mom hung tough Stateside, and it

would be a safe bet that Dad wrote to her every day over that two-year period. Just a few short years after the war, my big brother, also named Jack, came along. I was born in 1958; weighing in at ten pounds, I became the pride of the nursery.

Growing up in Grant County had advantages, although the downside was limited exposure to others. Our house, on Monroe Pike, was probably five miles from anywhere significant, but it had no bearing on the love my family shared early on. Life is funny in that the perception by one person can influence so many others. My impression of our family was that of the "Ozzie and Harriet" show from the 1950s. Dad was the dutiful provider. Mom was the stay-at-home, loving mother of two. She disciplined us, kept us on a schedule, and made sure we were polite and respectful.

Dad was very protective of his bride. He always put Mom on a pedestal. He told us he'd kick our butts if he ever heard us call her "the old lady." The 1960s were difficult for Dad because he clung to old-school beliefs. Change wasn't easy for him. Long hair was out and hippies didn't do anything but upset him. America was sacred along with the flag, the president, and anything that wasn't Chinese. Those feelings carried over from Korea.

Dad was always pushed to do more by my mother. He worked three jobs for a while, so the time spent with Jack and me was limited but precious. Dad took a job with Dana Corporation in 1964. His position required him to work from 3:00 p.m. to 11:00 p.m. The hours were not his first choice; however, the position offered him the chance to advance in the lab. One of his duties was to test the strength of metals like cast iron and steel. He absolutely loved the people he worked with, even the supervisor. Dad learned how to run the furnaces, which were used to strengthen the parts for machining. It was that knowledge he gained which brought about his biggest advancement. Dana relocated us to Lima, Ohio, in 1970 so that Dad could set up the lab at the newest facility in their Spicer Universal Joint Division. Brother Jack and I were at awkward ages for moving into a new school. I was twelve and in junior high. Jack was a freshman on his way to turning fifteen. New kids are normally not welcomed with open arms past the third grade or so. Acceptance wasn't something I remember happening overnight.

Living and growing up in the early 1970s was a trying time. So many things were different from the simple life in Grant County, Indiana. We lived outside Elida, Ohio, in a new housing area. We certainly weren't rich but some kids looked at us that way. Mom found work in real estate and soon had her license. However, the demand for showing a home after generally accepted working hours didn't seem to make her too happy, so selling houses faded. Mom was at her best running an office. She wound up at a staffing agency where she moved into the position of office administrator very quickly. There she made her mark as the very sharp lady whose retention was like a sponge. She snapped the office into an efficiently operating model for the rest of their locations to envy.

"Pride" was a word we heard and understood our whole lives. It still means a lot to me, but when pride is written about in the Bible, it doesn't have quite the same meaning. If you're familiar with how God feels about being prideful you know it can erode a person's clear thinking. As I said, the '70s brought on some choices that we all had to face. My brother made some of those life-altering decisions after he graduated from high school. He became a pawn in a political battlefield, and in 1975 he was facing time in jail. The district attorney at the time was bound and determined to set an example. Jack was truly in the wrong

7

place at the absolute worst time. Mom and Dad were mortified. They had just been punched in the face by the long arm of the law.

Jack had married in November of 1974. He had enlisted in the air force to learn heavy-machine operating. Every boy's dream is to drive a bulldozer, I guess. He was sent to Texas for basic training. Six weeks into his new career the authorities sent a few good men to extradite my brother from Lackland AFB in San Antonio, Texas, back to Lima, Ohio. Jack was brought home to face the charges filed against him. A tremendous burden had been laid on our family. The weight made it seem like we had been hit by a meteor. It sucked the pride out of our parents. As expected, my brother took it exceptionally hard. The proverbial rug had been jerked out from under all of us. I was sixteen at the time. Jack had had a huge influence on a lot of *my* decisions. We hung out together and even had mutual friends.

Along with life's struggles and difficulties come acquaintances and influential people. One of my father's brothers worked for the US government. Uncle Fred was a postal facility inspector. He had been introduced to some of those powerful folks. It was due to some of Fred's persistent pushing, phone calls, and bulldog attitude that the court system decided to let my brother serve his sentence under a program called shock probation. He was put back to work at Dana Corp but never could lift his head up quite as high. Dad was right behind him with encouragement and support. Outwardly, Dad was just as proud of his sons as ever before. I know inside it was eating him alive. The trauma had taken a toll on all of us.

After graduating high school, I became the newest UAW member through my employment with Dana Corporation. The position was a mindless grind from 3:00 p.m. to 11:00 p.m. There's not much thought behind unloading then reloading and cycling a machine all night. The pay and benefits were very competitive for the time, but I wasn't too satisfied with my life. I had allowed myself to drift some from our family.

I never kept God too far from my thoughts, though, and in late 1976, I distinctly remember praying for someone to come into my life who would complement me as a loving spouse. If you are a believer, you fully understand that we are not on the same calendar with our wishes and prayers as our Lord and Savior. It was not until May of 1978 that a little lady came along. Like a bolt of lightning, she took me by surprise. She was independent, spunky, and took no prisoners. Thirty-two years later, Sheryl—or as the family calls her, Sheri—is still a tremendous part of my life and proud mother of our children Todd, Trisha, and Tyler. My family stands as proof that the power of prayer is very real.

Chapter Two

Change of Scenery

ALL GOOD THINGS COME TO an end. The high inflation years of the late 1970s had created the need for Dana to lay some people off. In May of 1980, the downturn showed its effect on me. The reduction in force didn't really hurt at first. Trisha was four months old, and since Todd was five going on six, he was fairly low-maintenance. We had a great summer together. The free time gave me the chance of a lifetime to be directly involved in bonding with and raising our two children. Unemployment plus a supplement from the union gave us about ninety percent of my weekly pay. Sheri worked during the day at a deli. She was paid a very competitive hourly wage.

October of that same year brought around a life-altering event. My unemployment would run out in less than a month, and in our area there were no jobs. There was no way, in my mind, for us to make it financially. My brother approached me about an invitation Dana had made to assist its family of employees through a relocation program. The choices of available jobs were Chicago; Bridgeport, Connecticut; and Wichita Falls, Texas. Once Jack and I got to Texas, it was the clear winner. We both found separate jobs on the same day.

The move was difficult for all of us. Trisha was a funny little ten-month-old, while Todd was a little man at six. My parents were very supportive, since they had experienced a transfer, but the distance was a killer. One thousand fifty miles is a long way to move at such a young age. I was just twenty-two, and my loving little wife was just twenty-three.

It took only a year for Dad to decide relocation would be a great way to fix the long-distance challenge of seeing their grandchildren. Dad found a supervisor's position in Lancaster, just outside of Dallas. He and Mom moved in November of 1981 to Duncanville, Texas. The man of her dreams had come through again. Jack C. Pulley never thought twice about taking another risk by moving to an unfamiliar area. This was just his way of trying to please Mom. He always strived to make her as happy as she could be.

True to form, Mom landed a position with the City of Duncanville. She soon became well-liked, not only for her personality, but also for her efficiency and professionalism. Pat Pulley thrived at helping with early voting, coordinating the office, and trying to make the whole system run smoothly. She always took pride, plus some ownership, in the positions she held. Mom felt like the people she worked around were an extended part of her own family. She handled the payroll for the entire city, which included the fire department as well as the police. The City of Duncanville's newest employee soon was known throughout the system as a likeable individual with a sharp wit. To top it all off, she was attractive for her age.

The four years from 1981 to 1985 were solid for Mom. She and Dad had a beautiful home with a pool, along with good friends and neighbors. Living closer to their grandkids proved to be another plus. We would travel to visit my parents four to six weekends per summer. The grandkids would enjoy their time in Grandpa's pool. Dad relished his role as ringleader. He always made a point of having plenty to eat for our gang. His grandkids, especially Trisha, could do no wrong.

I had just started a new job in our town of Iowa Park, Texas. Cryovac had assigned me to work the day shift. The weather was clear and sunny on that February morning, the eighteenth. The world had just blossomed in 1986. I was enjoying a new job, good health—everything was looking positive.

Dad had essentially been forced into early retirement by an aggressive plant manager. From what we gathered, he needed an opening for a friend who just so happened to have the qualifications to fill Dad's position. The company Dad had sacrificed so much of his life for had, in turn, sacrificed Jack C. Pulley.

Around 9:30 in the morning, my dad died of a massive heart attack. He was gone before he hit the garage floor. Fifty-three years is what God had blessed him with. The blessing was all ours, in ways we may never understand. His influence on me still shows itself on a daily basis.

Mom was only fifty years old. She had only ever known Dad as her lover, friend, and husband. They had been happily married since June 7, 1952, until that February morning of 1986. Jack and Pat had actually dated since Mom was only fourteen, so my mother hadn't been in any type of single situation since 1949. I still feel an empty sensation in the pit of my stomach when I think back to that time of our lives.

Chapter Three

Revising a Lifestyle

I CAN STILL SEE MOM AT her front door after the funeral, when all the family had gone, telling Jack and me to go home. "I'll be fine," she kept saying. I think we were all still in shock. My memory of our two-hour drive home is limited, but I can recall feeling like I was floating. Upon my return to work, I was not concentrating well. I cannot imagine how Mom kept her focus, either.

The rest of the 1980s saw Mom struggling to discover who she was and what made her happy. Sometimes it was painful when dealing with her sharp remarks, as if Jack or I had done something awful to her. Her anger at Dad dying seemed to consume her. Our visits became less frequent. Mom found some kind of comfort in phone conversations with our daughter. Trisha always seemed older beyond her years; however, nine is a little young to have a conversation with an adult. The two started talking on a regular basis in late 1989.

Loneliness is almost a silent killer. Mom had grown up in a very busy household. The only time she had spent away from Dad was while he was in Korea. Even then she and my Uncle Fred's wife, Shirley, lived together while both of their husbands were away. The adjustment to single life never really took shape.

Just before Dad passed away, his youngest sister, Susan, moved to Texas. She arrived only a few weeks before he died. Aunt Susan was a slim, dark-haired, attractive woman. She was very thoughtful and intelligent. No one ever questioned why Dad had opened his home to his sister. Susan's life had changed since she divorced, and she had come to big brother Jack's looking for a fresh start. She had no idea what kind of lifestyle she was about to experience.

After Dad's passing, Susan decided to stay with Mom for a while to try to give her support. Susan became Mom's sounding board. Mom didn't know how to handle another woman in her house. The two never really got along during the time my aunt lived there. People use different outlets for comfort after suffering the loss of someone close. There are support groups, books, prayer, or a trusted friend. Mom turned to drinking vodka very regularly. Susan would stop by the liquor store every other day and pick up a half-gallon jug.

Mom minimized Dad's death by referring to it as "Jack's situation." She even went to the extreme of making Susan sleep in the same bed with her. Normally, Susan would just wait until she fell asleep, then she would get up to go into the guest room. There were quite a few nights Susan got up to find Mom in Dad's closet beating on his clothes with both fists while sobbing. Most of the time, she would let Susan console her until she settled down, but there were occasions where her outbursts would turn to rage. Mom would grab Susan by the wrists with a firm grip. These out-of-control emotional moments made Susan feel as if it were her fault.

Mom was trying to replace Dad with Aunt Suse. She had Susan drive her wherever she wanted to go. She would make her fill up the car at the gas station. Mom also insisted that she take the Olds through the car wash. Once, Susan even tried to force Mother out of the car at the filling station to show her how to use the pump. Mom simply refused to get out. Ignoring Susan, she just sat in the passenger seat staring straight ahead. Susan made the comment that she was not Jack. She was adamant about Mom becoming more independent.

Dad had always told her that if something ever happened to him, the men would come knocking down the door. She constantly asked Susan, "Where are they?"

Aunt Susan found a position with Loftland Steel in Dallas. Employment equaled freedom for Suse; it allowed her to find a place of her own. During this time, Susan had one of her daughters in town for a visit. Mom's relentless hounding pushed both Susan and her daughter Lori to the brink. Susan rented an apartment within a week of Lori's arrival. The two of them actually slept on the floor the first night, since Susan had no furniture.

Mom wasn't completely alone. She had her only brother, John, who lived in Red Oak, Texas. This sleepy little town was about forty-five minutes from Duncanville. John became her handy man, confidant, and her new replacement for the void left after Dad passed. Susan had moved on, so Mom didn't have anyone in her house. John did everything from cleaning gutters to replacing light bulbs. At one time, I considered John one of my favorite uncles. He was tough. He normally wore a mustache. He had worked construction most of his life, and being outside had given his face a weathered look. I would say he had that "Burt Reynolds" look about him. The palms of his hands were normally calloused from handling brick or cinderblocks. His frame was average, but you could tell he wasn't one to mess with.

Mom sweetened the pot by letting John use Dad's light utility pickup truck. My uncle, however, had his own family. Mom's calls at all hours became a source of frustration for Uncle John and his wife, Barb. John and Barb had two young children, Patrick and Jennifer, and spending time with their family was precious to them both. Mom had allowed her loneliness to carry over into selfishness. The damage she inflicted was starting to be felt around my house.

I love my family, so when I began getting wind of some serious discontent from my aunt and uncle, my hands were all but tied. We lived over two hours from Duncanville. A road trip on a regular basis was entirely out of the question. I worked a revolving twelve-hour shift. Every other weekend was taken by work, not to mention having all three of our own children in soccer, baseball, football, basketball, plus track, piano lessons, and dance. Life truly goes on, and our lifestyle was no exception. We stayed very active with the kids' schedules. Sheri and I wanted to give our children every opportunity to try as many activities as possible.

Without realizing it, Mom was slowly living her life more and more alone. She hadn't intentionally driven family away but the harsh reality was just that. She couldn't clone Jack C. Pulley. No way could she recreate the man who had been there all of her adult life. The one person who could keep her outbursts under control and love her like no one else, had been taken in a flash. Dad had placed her on a delicate pedestal of respect, love, and constant attention. Gone were the moments of his irreplaceable, intimate affection. At the age of fifty, it all came to a crashing halt.

Mom never recovered. Over a period of four years, she dated guys who couldn't hold a candle to the man she had entrusted her love to.

She was a million miles from anything familiar. She didn't have any idea who to reach out to or how to begin putting a new life back into place. Her pride and persistence were telling her she could handle it. Mom refused to believe she could not get herself back on track. She took on an "everything-is-fine" attitude. Pat refused to ask anyone for help.

As I mentioned, Mom had a brother, John. She also had four sisters: Shirley, Carolyn, Cathy, and Jeanne. Mom was the oldest, but Shirley was only a couple of years younger. Throughout their lives, they remained close. Shirley lived in California, so their visits usually came in the form of long phone conversations or letters. This was well before any instant-messaging technology. Shirley kept her faith through her relationship with God. She was a good lady and Mom's closest ally.

Mom didn't have many friends, especially the kind you can really talk to, by which I mean the kind of people who will listen with an open heart. Mom didn't have the type of folks who, even if they didn't understand, would still listen out of pure support. Her personal ship was sinking. Mother's work never suffered, because that was her extended family. The office became the only outlet she knew. She had counseled once or twice with the chaplain of the fire department, who had done a nice job of performing the service for Dad's funeral. True to her personality, Mom didn't allow the chaplain to get too close. Nothing concrete ever came from her counseling with him.

Life can become a grind. Get up, go to work, take your lunch, finish up your day, and then go home at 5:00. Some go home to an empty house, which can become familiar but unsatisfying. My mother had enjoyed sharing her day with Dad. Most evenings they would visit, eat a light dinner, and then just sit together to watch television.

My dad was a Texas Rangers fan, so he and Mom would go to a game in Arlington on occasion. Mom didn't knit, go to craft shows, or take a lot of time reading. Dad did the yard work, plus he kept the pool clean. Every Sunday, Dad would take Mom's car to fill it up with gas as well as run it through the car wash. I remember once, after he died, Mom had gone to the convenience store by herself. She sat and cried because she couldn't find that "damn" gas cap. Whenever she would tell that story, she laughed about crying. I am sure that down deep the loneliness was creeping like a cancer throughout her system.

Chapter Four

California Dreamin'

B Y NOVEMBER OF 1989, MOM had reached a point in her life where there was no turning back. Patricia L. Pulley had had enough. She had become thoroughly fed up with the life she was living. The destitution created by Dad's death set her on a mission that would rock my family's world.

She planned a trip to California to visit her sister Shirley. The two hadn't seen one another for quite some time. Mom was down deep in the dumps and she may have had finding a partner on her mind. Not long after arriving in California, Shirley, her husband Dick, and Mom had reservations at a restaurant on the beach. Well, the word *reservation* in California must mean, "You'll still wait until we have a table," because the three of them were directed downstairs to the cocktail lounge. From Shirley's account, the minute they walked through the door, Mom hesitated. She whispered to Shirley that she saw a man who looked like Jack.

It is really hard to explain this fellow Mom saw. If you watch professional football, you may know of a coach named Jimmy Johnson, whose hair was always in place. It's a good way to describe the man Mom spotted that night. Mom and this man danced in the club and exchanged telephone numbers. After dinner, Mom was as excited as a little school girl over this clown.

Upon her return to Texas, the long-distance relationship began, mostly through letters, though I am sure she phoned him more than I care to know. Mom had shown me a letter he had written that included a cheesy Polaroid picture of her new Casanova. The hand-written letter is still clear in my mind. He had scribbled his message on yellow legal paper. Some words were misspelled. The grammar he used was very simple. My first impression was not positive; however, some individuals don't express themselves well in writing, so I tried to be supportive.

In all of Mom's newfound exuberance, she lost contact with reality and sound judgment. In a rush to put an end to her old way of life, she sent her Californian a Visa Gold credit card. His instructions were to take his time, but he should start heading to Texas. After a few stops for clothes, a belt, boots, and gas for his piece-of-crap Oldsmobile, the West Coast Wonder showed up in the Lone Star State. On April 6, 1990, James Reginald Massey hit the front door.

Massey was a self-absorbed, boisterous loudmouth. He stood about five feet ten inches tall. His weight was about right for his frame. He was fidgety and never had anything positive to say. He would look at you as if it was a huge inconvenience for you to be around. From his soft appearance, it was obvious he had never put in a solid day's work. Most of his efforts, it seemed, were put toward making himself look just right.

During better times, one of my dad's joys in life was to have us come down to spend the weekend, usually around the pool. We would all stay until Sunday afternoon before heading back home. Those weekends were very relaxing. The time we had together, albeit too short, was always memorable. One of the first things on my parents' priority list would be to call Pizza Inn to place an order to go. We always used coupons to get the biggest bang for our buck. You couldn't go wrong feeding three children—well, four, counting me—with plenty of pizza after swimming all day. Dad always made sure of two things: First, he made sure Mom was happily set up. Mom never learned to swim, so when we all went to the pool, she generally kept her distance. Second, he made sure to keep his camera clicking, taking plenty of pictures.

Massey, the West Coast Wonder, had arrived in Texas. For reasons not clear at the time, we hadn't been invited for a visit to Mom's until late June. Mom finally called to have us all rush down to meet her savior. She was ramped up with anticipation over our visit. I know my tone is sarcastic, but from the beginning, I was very skeptical. I tried to be supportive, positive, and open-minded to this newly discovered "best-thing-since-sliced-bread" acquaintance.

The big moment arrived. We all made our way into the kitchen to greet this guy for the very first time. Mom was visually nervous. I could see she was nearly holding her breath. I wasn't expecting to meet anyone like my dad; I honestly never dreamed that I would. After a brief introduction, Massey stuck out his hand, and I reached to shake, as any well- intentioned grown man would do. What I grabbed was a baby-soft, wet rag. This guy had no firm grip. He seemed put out that we had taken the time to show up.

The next step was to get the kids in the pool and order some food. Following family tradition, the coupons were out on the counter by the phone. Once our order had been taken, I gave the fellow my last name,

Pulley, then hung up.

Massey looked at me and asked, "What name did you put the order under?"

I told him, "Pulley."

He looked at me and said, "Give me the number of the pizza place." His voice was bold and cocky.

Man, I have to say, I was confused as I gave him the phone number. Without hesitating, Massey called the Pizza Inn. While looking at me, he told the guy the order that just came in under the name Pulley was to be changed to Massey. He had to tell the employee two or three times. It was so ridiculous that none of us, including my mother, could believe this was happening. We had only been around Massey for about forty-five minutes.

Once he was off the phone, my wife looked him in the eye and said, "You are an asshole."

My wife walked out to the pool, and Mom nervously lit a cigarette. She tried to blow off Massey's little show. "He's just a big joker," she said. Words couldn't justify what the rest of our time there was like. He tried to outsmart me, talk down to me, and compare what he had done with what I had accomplished. Looking back, I now know this was one method of alienating outside family and influences. He hadn't been in Mom's house more than two months, but the wheels of control had already started turning. We all had a lot to learn. Tragically, none of us realized we had just been given a lesson in abuse. This was foreign territory for the Pulley family.

When spring 1991 came around, Mom and Massey ran off to Reno, Nevada, for a private wedding. No one was told until after the ceremony. I honestly can't think of anyone who would have gone if they had been invited. Massey was so full of himself, it sickened everyone—I truly mean *everyone*—who was around him.

Mom had fallen victim to a man she hadn't allowed herself enough time to know or understand. She was discovering some of his unique personality traits. Perhaps she thought some might change when, in fact, she had changed to conform to *his* actions. He job-hopped quite a bit. He was a big-talking used car salesperson. I know some honorable people in the car business. I also know guys like Massey who are in the business for a reason. Waking your body up with orange juice and vodka may not be starting your day with the breakfast of champions. Mom never stepped back to consider any of the consequences. She was forcing her acceptance of their lifestyle to accommodate him since he was *her* find, her responsibility.

Pride is not something you should allow to rule clear thinking. Mom's prideful ways told her to take this situation and own it. She had chosen to bring this loser home from the West Coast. She was overlooking his obvious ignorant behavior and laziness. His drinking got worse. I'm sure he had found a local connection for the cocaine, pot, or whatever else he was drowning in.

Uncle John and Barb found themselves smack dab in the middle of Massey's controlling personality. John was always directly involved with both of their children's activities. He was coaching seven-year-old Patrick in T-Ball. Patrick was a little base-burning, aggressive athlete. John and Barb had encouraged Mom and Massey to attend a game. After all, family should get out to enjoy, support, and cheer for a great group of young children. It's encouraging to see them trying their best to learn the game while having fun.

In Texas, it turns pretty hot in late May. That is about the time Mom and Massey decided to take John and Barb up on their invitation. Since it was only about a forty-five minute drive to Red Oak, it wasn't a long trip to see Patrick play. Once the hour-long game ended, Mom went on to start the car so the A/C could begin cooling things down. Massey stayed behind, turned his back to the car, and called John over.

Allow me to clarify a couple of things. Uncle John had never really warmed up to James Massey. John's goal was to keep things civil for his big sister. Also, this was the first time the two had really been apart from Mom.

Massey looked at John and said, "Don't you ever do this to us again."

John was surprised. "Do what?"

"Make us come to one of these f------ ball games in the heat." Massey turned and walked toward the car. Before he got in, he wheeled around. "I'll see you later," he said with a smile and a wave.

Later that same summer, Massey's youngest daughter, Jamie, came to visit from Florida. She had a baby girl to show to Grandpa. My family had actually made the trip, only to please Mom. We were all standing in the kitchen when Jamie and her newborn came in from the airport. Massey was as goofy as the Disney character.

Turning to me, Jamie looked confused and asked me, "Is he always this way?"
Biting my tongue to spare Mom from too much grief, I simply replied,

"He's your dad."

Not surprisingly, our visit at Mom's wasn't a long one. James was so unbearably childlike in his comments and smothering performance toward his daughter, it made leaving very easy. Jamie didn't mind staying. She was getting all the attention, plus everything she needed was provided by Mom.

Massey turned his sights toward Red Oak. He wanted John and Barb to come see his new grandchild. John worked long hours, and it was not uncommon for him to get home late. Plus, he was not fond of J. R. Massey. From conversations I had with John, his enthusiasm for making a trip to see the new arrival was just to the left of zero. Barb was always polite. The decision to see his grandchild had been left up to John.

After a dozen or more persistent calls from Massey, Barb said to John, "Go ahead."

I realize most readers of this book have had no exposure to John Montgomery during moments like this; if you had, then you'd know what was next. Once John had Massey on the phone, all his restraint was unleashed. It was a loud, profanity-filled, five-minute burst of absolute disdain for the person Mom had gone off to Reno with and married. John fully intended to make it very clear that neither he nor any member of his family had a care in the world about seeing Massey's new grandchild.

Uncle John finally let up long enough for Massey to simply say, "Okay," and he just hung up.

Several weeks went by before an unexpected knock came at John and

Barb's door. Mom and James had shown up on a Saturday morning. Uncle John was seated at the kitchen table, still eating breakfast, when the two came in. Without saying a word, James sat down next to John, reached over, grabbed his plate of food, and moved it over in front of himself, then began eating Uncle John's breakfast. I'm sure John was ready to hurt him in a very violent manner. Luckily for James, Barb was there to prevent John from erupting. John told me he simply encouraged Massey to leave and never come back. Mom tried defending Massey. She told John that would include her as well.

Sadly, all John could say was, "Well, Pat, if that's the way you want it, then that is the way it will have to be."

I believe this was just another of Massey's moves to further distance family from Mom. Pat Massey was on an island which wasn't inhabited by friendly natives. Hindsight tells us what J. R. Massey was doing. Loneliness, bitterness, and desperation were driving Mom to force herself to stand by her vicious spouse. He hadn't held a job for more than a month or two since arriving in Texas, yet he never had a problem spending Mom's money. He had controlled our first meeting with his tasteless phone call to the pizza place to change the last name on our order to *his* last name. He slowly positioned John and Barb to despise him. Making matters worse, Mom had gone to the extent of choosing *him* over her own brother. The decision put Massey in even more control over Mom.

Since Massey insisted on always answering the phone when it rang, my calls became less frequent. The only time Mom called was when he was not in the house. Those phone calls usually lasted less than an hour. My aunts Cathy and Carolyn made the same comment. They could rarely speak to her for long because as soon as he came in the house she would whisper, "I have to go."

Chapter Five

Indiana Wants Me

JOHN AND BARB HAD HAD enough of the lack of employment opportunities in their industries. They packed up and headed home to Indiana. Grandpa Montgomery's health wasn't good, so being closer to his parents became urgent. The decision for John to go back to the Hoosier State was easy. January of 1992 brought around a further decline in Grandpa's health. Mom's father passed away in February.

During the time James allowed Mom to stay after her father's funeral, he was his usual silly self. He was always trying to hit on the women. His presence alone irritated the whole family. Mom had let her guard completely down, even when it came to her family. James had met Mom's little sister, Jeanne, during the funeral. Now here was Jeanne, a mature woman, and Mom let Massey refer to her as B. J. for "Big Jugs." Mom didn't say anything. As a matter of fact, she laughed about it as if it was fine for him to degrade her own sister.

It wasn't long before Mom and Massey were back in Texas. That year, James Massey got a DWI and a night in jail for shoplifting at a local Tom Thumb grocery store. His drinking was steady, and so was his abuse. He even showed up at the City of Duncanville offices during the day. I understand from those who witnessed this disturbing show,

James told everyone who could hear him that his wife was overworked. He went on to say she planned on taking all the time off that the city would allow. He made her get up and leave that very moment. Because of these types of antics, Mom was demoted. This was all new territory for her. The humiliation was mortifying. Uncharacteristically, her work suffered.

For the next several months, James would leave little gifts around the house. During a few conversations with Mom, she told me she felt these were attempts at redeeming himself for his immature outbursts. This was viewed by Mom as a step toward positive personal change. She had put up with insults, physical and mental abuse, plus public embarrassment at the hands of an ice-cold spouse.

Mom had no one to confide in. She turned to my daughter, Trisha, who had just turned thirteen. The two had talked some since she was nine but this level of discussion was a little advanced for someone so young. Some topics of their talks dealt with Mom being unhappy in her relationship. She spoke of some minor abuse. Mom confided that she was trying to find a way out. This was a very heavy burden to place on Trisha; however, through Mom's loss of friends and close family she apparently felt there was no one left to turn to. Massey regulated all of the incoming and outbound phone calls. If Grandma called her granddaughter, it may have seemed acceptable in his twisted mind. Their calls were not limited, nor were they interrupted.

The summer of 1993 brought the loss of Mom's mother. Grandma was the kindest, most gentle individual God ever placed on this good Earth, and Massey was griping about the cost of going to Indiana. Initially, he wasn't going to permit Mom to attend the funeral. This became the family wake-up call. Mother's sisters called to give him a firm piece of their minds. We were all upset. After all his ignorant displays, even this shocked us. How could he think of not letting her go? With a push from all of the family, James finally agreed to let Mom attend her own mother's funeral.

With her credit pushed to the limit, Mom somehow found the resources to fly home. This was one of the few times she was not accompanied by her no-class husband. The scars he had left on Mom's entire family were too deep. My guess would be he had chosen not to come along due to the reception he would have gotten from John. Aunt Carolyn informed me that Mom constantly phoned home just to "check in" with Massey. No one could understand how she had allowed such a disrespectful, arrogant bum into our family.

Later that same year, I had planned a trip to Dallas with all three of our kids. I say kids even though Todd had turned nineteen, Trisha was thirteen, and Tyler was just shy of twelve. I can still see us getting out of the car.

James was at the front door. He took a look at Todd and asked, "Who is he?" He was so out of touch with Mom's family he hadn't taken the time to even know her own grandchildren.

Todd and I had plans that night. Trisha and Tyler stayed at the house while we took in an event. We got home late, and then got up early. All four of us were ready to escape what was becoming an unbearable atmosphere. This all fell right into his plan of eliminating all outside contacts, placing him in total control. It was demoralizing and I could see the toll it was taking on Mom.

Some might be thinking that they would have taken matters into their own hands by pulling him outside to put a little "Texas justice" in play. Believe me, that thought had passed through my mind a hundred times. I also came to realize that it was Mom's decision to live this way. If I *had* forced myself on him, two things could have happened, both negative. One would be the further distance it would have placed between me and Mom. Second, I was confident that a lawsuit would have followed any physical altercation.

I am not an aggressive person; however, this was my five-foot-two mother. This puffed up, controlling, alcohol-sponge had abused her in a variety of ways, probably some we'll never be made aware of. Suppressing thoughts of violence is more like a volcano than we realize. Eruptions are never timely and always messy, heated, and permanent. My personal life was being affected. Nightmares of striking J. R. Massey, Louisville Slugger in hand, with numerous adrenaline-pumped snaps of my wrists jerked me out of a dead sleep more than once. Short, snappy comments came from my mouth before I had time to think. Once words are out, you can never pull them back. Worry, frustration, and helplessness were only a portion of how I was feeling toward Mom's predicament. Every person in our family had been forced outside of Mom's life. Now we waited to see what was going to happen next on the "inside."

Mom was spending her weekdays at work until five, then coming home to James. He was always unpredictable. His mood was never the same. Her life was filled with a depressive atmosphere with no one to reach out to. Mom was a believer in Christ, so I'm sure she prayed for an answer. She spent some of her Sundays talking with our daughter Trisha. Part of those conversations included her unhappiness. She was looking for a way out of her current lifestyle. Trisha was not a typical teen. She never shared the fact that she was becoming Grandma's counselor. I feel Trisha understood that Mom needed an outlet, so she actually did more listening than talking.

Chapter Six

Looking Over the Edge

THE FALL OF 1993 BROUGHT around several changes. Our oldest was off at college. Sheri and I stayed busy with the other two kids. Trisha was active in eighth grade sports. Tyler competed in football, basketball, and baseball.

January 1, 1994, was like any other New Year's Day in our house. Todd was home from school, and we were in front of the TV enjoying as many football games as we could channel-surf through. Around 2:30 in the afternoon, the phone rang. It was Mom. Instantly, I knew she had been drinking. I could hear in her voice there was something very, very wrong.

With her speech a little slurred she said, "That S.O.B beat me up. He pushed me down in the kitchen, and I think he really hurt me. I can barely stand up."

I tried to compose myself as my grip tightened around the phone. As my anger spiked, I asked, "Where is he?"

Mom replied, "He's passed out on the couch." There was so much anger in her voice I could feel it coming through the phone. She went on to say, "He made me make him something to eat after he attacked me. Then he went into the living room and passed out."

Carefully, I thought before I spoke. My hands were wet with sweat and my voice shaking. My heart was pounding and I had a vision of uncontrolled violence toward this person who, in a drunken rage, had now beaten my mother.

"Okay, Mom, I'll come to your house under a couple of conditions. When I get there, you are going to file a restraining order, change the locks on every door, and file for divorce."

I then explained that I would no longer live a hypocritical life. If she allowed him back in the house, I would never step foot in it again. She did not hesitate when she agreed.

The first thing I grabbed was a twenty-seven-inch aluminum baseball bat. My wife, Sheri, was starting to panic. She hurriedly asked Todd to get ready and go with me. Her goal was for Todd to restrain me from really doing some serious damage. Too late—I was gone out the front door. I was heading out to pick up my brother Jack.

Two and a half hours of windshield time can really settle a guy down. I felt it was critical to stop by the Duncanville Police Department before heading into a violent release of my anger and frustration. I had no idea what I was going to find when I got to Mom's house. I do remember the first thing on my mind was to hit this guy as hard as I could, somewhere around the shins, just to get it started.

Jack and I flew up to the entrance at the police station. Like most big law enforcement facilities, the public cannot get in after a certain hour on the weekend. This was New Year's Day, early evening on a Saturday. My pending volcanic eruption was placing an enormous amount of pressure behind my eyes. Jumping out of my truck, I ran up to the window, held the button impatiently, and waited for the attendant's response. After it had buzzed a few seconds, there came a female voice on the other side.

She sounded a little put-out that someone had interrupted her late afternoon. Within my mind I had a vision of the employee. I could see her reading a magazine, feet propped up, and waiting for the clock to strike five. "May I help you?" Her voice was emotionless.

"Yes, my mother has been beaten by her so-called husband." I felt my face become beet red with fury. "If you all don't get a squad car to 215 Hillcroft you're gonna find him in a heap."

Now that got a response! "Now sir, there is no reason to be so belligerent!" she came back excitedly.

"Look, my mom is Pat Massey. I know you know her, so get someone out there or I'll handle this by myself!"

I was done. I leaped back in the truck, where I noticed Jack was a little pale. We whipped out of the station toward Mom's house. Immediately, I spotted two squad cars flying down Main Street, and I fell right in behind them. We hit sixty miles per hour down the middle of Duncanville, but I didn't care. Jack was pleading with me to slow down. There was no chance of me backing off now.

Mom only lived a couple miles from the police station. In just minutes, we were pulling up in front of the house. I felt invincible as I jumped out of the truck. Fists clenched, jaws locked in anger, I stormed in right behind the officers. They told me two or three times, "Get back in your vehicle, sir." Anxiety overtook me while I stood beside the truck, watching, as they cautiously approached the house. The porch light went out just as the two got to the front door step. I thought, *What an idiot. Massey turns off the lights with two fully-trained professional city police officers three steps from knocking on the door.*

They hit the solid wood door with their night sticks loudly, exclaiming, "Open up! This is the police!"

It is so cliché, but I distinctly remember telling one of the officers to just give me five minutes with Massey. It would save them a whole lot of time. As soon as the door was opened, they instantly cuffed him. Massey was so drunk he staggered uncontrollably down the sidewalk. I had slowly made my way closer through Mom's front yard until I was only ten feet away from the porch. I could have spit on him, I was so close. This pathetic, slobbering lump had no clue that I was standing right there. There was little satisfaction watching the officers put him in the backseat of the squad car. It could have been twenty degrees below zero, and I wouldn't have known.

The entire chain of events moved surreally. Some of it seemed in slow motion while other parts of the day sped by. It felt like I was strapped to a chair and couldn't reach out to get my hands around Massey's neck to stop his arrogant, abusive attacks on my very own mother. I had an empty gut-wrenching knot in my stomach from knowing Mom was allowing her life to become such an unbearable hell. No one in the family could stand to hear Massey's voice, much less be around him. This was nothing like the life Jack C. Pulley had created for his bride of thirty-five years. There had always been love, laughter, and plenty of hugs to go around. No one was ever intimidated or embarrassed by my father. He was kind and funny and a loving partner to Mom.

My attention turned back to the front door. Mom's silhouette became visible as she gingerly leaned on the frame. As my brother and I approached, she began to cry. It was the kind of release that you have when something has been tucked away for a very long time. The light from inside the living room hit her face. James had beaten her beyond recognition. As she tried to catch her breath, she apologized for all of the trouble she'd caused. The only thing we kept telling her was to sit down. All of her makeup had been erased from her sunken face. It quickly became obvious she was in a tremendous amount of pain.

The house was a mess, which was out of the norm for our mother. The stench of booze and cigarettes caught me right in the throat. Once inside, I spotted a ten-inch knife on the coffee table. The blade glistened in the pale light. The weapon had been pulled out of its sheath. This tool of soldiers had been laid out for all to see. The only use for a knife like this was for killing or maiming a person. The blade had a pronounced jagged edge on top, and a razor-sharp cutting edge. In the middle of the table were paper plates. The plates held the leftover bits and pieces of snack food. Incredibly, Massey found it acceptable to munch while he beat the hell out of Mom.

In between crying and blubbering, Mom explained that Massey had threatened to kill *me* with the knife. So on top of kicking her around that night, he also planted the thought that I was going to die just for showing up. It was all-too-familiar trash-talking from a guy who could barely put one foot in front of the other as the police hauled him away. This was just another of his small-minded ways of making Mom his puppet. Control her with fear. His relentless mental battering had led Mom to fund his nonstop drinking. She had even given him money to blow on movies during the day while *she* worked. With the exception of giving him access to her accounts, Mom had done just about everything she was able to do financially.

Jack and I had seen enough. Mom had back surgery on her lower lumbar in 1985. Now, we were both very concerned, because she continued to show signs of trauma in that same area. Once we got her settled down, I realized we had to take her to the emergency room. During all of this confusion, I think we took time to call my wife to let her know some of the details. This was well before the era of a cell phone in everyone's pocket. We hurriedly used the house phone before we left.

The real rush was over. We were not relaxed by any stretch of the imagination, but an unusual calm came over me. We made good time on our way to the hospital. I reminded Mom of our deal. She was going to file charges and *not* drop them. She knew good attorneys who could get a divorce moving along quickly. She needed to get a restraining order, plus change the locks on every door. As we all know, these are basic measures a lot of people have taken; however, none of them would guarantee her safety.

Our trip to the emergency room seemed to take forever. I am sure it had to be extremely painful for Mom. Once we arrived we got her checked in and the wait began. Jack and I finally got her into an exam room. She continued telling us she was sorry. Repeatedly she would say, "Everything is going to be fine."

The doctor came in, took one look at Mom, turned to *me* and demanded, "What happened here?" His look cut right through me. He had that glare, as if he was thinking I had done the unspeakable.

I cleared that thought from his mind in an instant. "This is our mom. We have her here because of what her husband has done." I then went on to tell him that I wanted all of her wounds documented and filed. Something was telling me that someday we might need to access those records.

Once the X-rays came back, it was discovered that when Massey had shoved her down onto the kitchen floor, the force of her fall had broken her tailbone. So there was my mom, at fifty-eight years old, in a hospital, with black eyes and a broken tailbone. Massey had thrown her across the kitchen seven times. He had beaten her head on the floor and countertop. The thought of living two and a half hours away made it more difficult to accept the fact that, at some point, we had to go home. We knew James Massey couldn't be held in jail forever; plus, he had a stranglehold on Mom's emotions.

On the ride back to her house, I took a very gentle approach. Mom had been bullied plenty by the useless piece of flesh she had chosen to marry. I felt a kind voice would be a welcome change. Jack and I encouraged her to talk to an attorney. We tried to instill in her the urgency to surround herself with good people she could trust. We could help insulate her from the abusive beast James R. Massey had become and rid her of his controlling, obnoxious behavior. After all, what use was an out-of-control, unemployed alcoholic with no sincerity in his soul? No one could imagine any reason for Mom to cling to such a pathetic animal. He was a fast-talking smart aleck who never had a positive thing to say about anyone other than himself. He had driven us away and caused major friction between Uncle John and Mom. He had disgusted my wife and me the very first time we met. His continued barrage of slanderous speech and unacceptable actions toward my family made it easy to dislike him.

Jack and I loaded up and headed for home around 3:00 a.m. Mom begged us to stay, but there was no way I was going to spend the night in that house. I know both of us felt the same way, or else I would have been outnumbered. I remember my brother snoring most of the way back to North Texas. All the way home, I kept reminding myself that I now had the responsibility of staying in touch with Mom. My plan was to call daily with encouragement for her to be strong and not give in to her abuser. Living so far away, I knew she didn't have a good defense system. Massey had created so many barriers that most people had severed all personal ties with Mom. Jack and I made it home around sunrise on Sunday morning.

Monday night, after work, I called Mom, and after we talked for a while she sounded very strong and determined to keep Massey in jail. I gently reminded her to follow through with what we had discussed on New Year's Day: file for divorce, get a restraining order in place, change the locks, and start a new life without him.

When I called the second night, she had a different tone. I was worried that she had spoken to her little jailbird. His cycle of abuse would have been to sweet-talk her once again. She told me that she had some sort of plan, but wouldn't give me any details. All the while, I was reminding her that none of my family would ever come to her house as long as Massey was living there.

Wednesday came, and she had caved in. I told her that if she wanted to see her grandchildren, she would have to come to our house. With a stern voice, I told her to *never* bring J. R. Massey with her. She agreed and sadly said she understood. On that Monday, January 3, 1994, James Massey was released from the Duncanville city jail. Within three weeks, all charges were dropped.

Watching my mother deteriorate right before my eyes is not something that is easy to talk about. You know as a parent, you do your best to advise and guide your children, but they make their *own* mistakes. Even though some of Mom's actions were childlike, your parents are not like your children. She first had been impressed by a smooth-talking, nice-looking man who had a flashy dance move or two. She had been alone and very vulnerable. Desperate to find a replacement for the huge hole in her life, she had unwittingly let her guard drop. This opened the door for another person to come in and control her.

Mom had always earned and retained the respect of her peers. I know the employees at the city felt strongly about her abilities. They had all been very supportive when Dad passed away. Their kindness was a comfort for us all. Now that she had entered into an abusive relationship, most of the people surrounding her at work had distanced themselves from her. Due to Massey's outbursts in the city offices, she had been demoted. She had also missed some work, which was not in her character whatsoever. She was spinning out of control. There was nothing anyone could do to change her situation with the exception of herself, Patricia L. Massey.

Some of us have tried changing people in our lives. One of the hardest lessons in life is learning that, as individuals, we seldom do change. As we grow older we tend to slow down some, but we remain essentially the same inside. The mystery to us all is how a seemingly headstrong, independent woman could live with such an abusive, disrespectful human as Massey turned out to be. There was, from the outside, no rational reason for Mom to love this person. He truly brought down everyone he met. He never showed an ounce of remorse for any of his actions. He was a braggart who couldn't back any of his wild-eyed claims. He was the brashest adult I had ever met. He had never shown my family any sign of interest in getting to know them as individuals. Our family's loving relationship had been strained to the point of no return. Woefully, I had resolved to accept the fact that I wouldn't see my mother in her home again. It truly seemed as though she had made up her mind to overlook all of the negative points and focus on one thing: Pat was no longer alone.

Two months went by without a word from Mom. One weekday afternoon the phone rang and it was her. She really didn't have good news but I know she felt as if it were a step in a new direction. James had entered a rehab facility. The location was about an hour away. Our family has some experience with placing loved ones into rehab centers. One positive for our family is that most are Christian-based. There is another point to be fully aware of: a person who enters rehab at the insistence of someone else is *not* ready for change. The responsibility to yourself and commitment are overwhelming to most who have been through the entire program. Massey was a whining, needy crybaby the whole time. He spent more time calling Mom to come get him than he did going to sessions. It had been a little over two weeks when, once again, Mom caved in and drove the distance to pick him up. No doubt, the center was probably relieved watching him hit the exit door. For the rest of 1994, there wasn't much in the way of news coming from Mom's life.

Chapter Seven

Up Close and Personal

M OM HAD KEPT A DAILY journal inside a day planner. The words written below are her own. I took every step I could to accurately recreate what she documented. Mom refers to James R. Massey as "Jim." The first two entries are speaking about my family and me.

1993

Saturday
December 18 *Had a great day with Jim, Sheri & kids. Exchanged gifts, went to lunch at Olive Garden.*

Sunday
December 19 *Early lunch w/Jim at Olive Garden*

Friday
December 24 *Went out shopping at 7:00 a.m. Breakfast in Desoto w/Jim– went to movie, saw "Mrs. Doubtfire."*

Saturday
December 25 *Had a great day w/Jack & kids. Beautiful gift*

exchange. Mathew was sick.
Monday
December 27 *Jim–drinking again.*

Tuesday
December 28 *Jim–D.A.*

Wednesday
December 29 *Jim came home about 6:30 p.m–worked, but had been drinking too much. He insisted I go out w/him–Gold Rush & Cutters. Bought Chinese food & brought it home. I was upset with his stupid lies he told at the bar. Moved to my new office today.*

Thursday
December 30 *Enjoyed getting adjusted to my new office today. Called Jim at 5 p.m. to remind him I was getting my hair set. He just got home & had been drinking. He went back to Cutters & drank for another hour. When I came home, he came in 5 min. later somewhat "toasted." I became angry about everything when he drinks the afternoon away. He went to bed at 7:50 p.m. Another night alone. When he drinks, which is 5 days out of 6, I have no one. This is no marriage.*

Friday
December 31 *He brought 2 bottles of wine and 1 bottle of Vodka home today for New Year's Eve. He had been drinking most of the day.*

1994

Saturday
January 1 *Jim started drinking wine first thing this morning: (5 glasses by 11:00 a.m.) Very drunk by evening and he beat me–black eye, threw me down on the kitchen floor, injured my tailbone, bruised my left shoulder, my hip, and chest. Badly bruised left wrist. I was hysterical–called my sons–they came with police. Jim was taken to D'Ville jail. Boys took me to hospital–tailbone cracked.*

Sunday
January 2 *Spent day on couch. Can hardly move. Family calling to tell me get rid of him. Jim was transferred to Lou Starret.*

Monday
January 3 *Cannot go to work. Too much pain–face looks horrible. Jim still in jail. Called his boss to bail him out. I'm not going to. Jim has made our marriage a living HELL because of his excessive drinking. It just keeps going downhill. He'll never change. He has hurt me for the last time. He got out of jail tonight, took a taxi to come home. He couldn't believe how bad I looked. He said he would do anything I wanted him to–leave or whatever. I'm numb–I really don't care. He stayed.*

Tuesday
January 4 *Supervisor said take the week off–get well. Have had a relapse of Bronchitis. Wish I could fall off the face of the earth. I hate my life. Jim went to work. I'm not at ease with him yet. I still can't believe he hurt me so badly–it has wrecked my emotional stability.*

Wednesday
January 5 *I'm miserable.*
Jim went to M.A.D.D. seminar tonight. DWI requirement.

Thursday
January 6 *Went to the doctor for Bronchitis. A shot, more antibiotics.*

Friday
January 7 *Same old shit.*

Saturday
January 8 *Got my hair cut. Sherry noticed my black eye. Bought Merle Norman makeup to cover black eye.*

Sunday
January 9 *Still hurt.*

Monday
January 10 *Went back to work. I know everyone noticed my black eye. I was uncomfortable and embarrassed. I don't deserve this.*

Thursday
January 20 *Jim surprised me this morning. He hired a cleaning lady to clean house. It looks great.*

Saturday
January 22 *Went shopping today w/Jim. Bought 3 pair slacks, new skirt, & new robe.*

Sunday

January 23 *Watched football on TV.*
Monday
January 24 *Went to Court w/Jim this morning. I'm going to drop charges, but cannot talk with Ass't D.A. until Mar. 9.*

Tuesday
January 25 *Jim went to Drunk Driving school tonight–part of DWI requirements. He brought Chinese dinner home for us.*

Wednesday
January 26 *Jim went to D.D. school again tonight. He brought Mexican dinner home.*
My eye not healed yet. Very aggravating.

Thursday
January 27 *Jim completed DWI school. Passed–got certificate. Received notice that Auto Insurance has been cancelled due to his DWI ticket.*

Saturday
January 29 *Laid on couch all day. Back is killing me.*

Sunday
January 30 *Went out for breakfast. Watched Super Bowl. Good day.*

Monday
January 31 *Jim went to Cutter's after work. Had 5 drinks! I couldn't believe it! He has rubbed "salt in my wounds." He went to sleep 7:00 p.m. This is not a good life for me.*

Tuesday
February 1 *Got my hair set after work. Jim was not home when I came in. By 8:00 p.m. he had not called. I packed his belongings, put them in the garage, set the security switch on garage door, put chair under door knob of front door–went to bed angry. He rang doorbell 1:50 a.m. in the morning. Had not been drinking (he said). I don't believe him. He will bury himself with his lies. (Also found a new pistol he had purchased and had not told me).*

Wednesday
February 2 *He put all of his belongings back. He keeps me in an emotional turmoil. Will it ever get better? And Supervisor at work keeps using me as her "whipping post."*

Thursday
February 3 *I went to Personnel Administrator about supervisor's attitude. He wanted to talk w/her but I decided she would turn on me moreso. Hopefully, I can handle what she "dishes out." Went to dentist–have gum infection–more antibiotics.*
Evening O.K

Friday
February 4 *"Cold shoulder" treatment again from Supervisor.*
Evening O.K.
Dad passed away 2 yrs ago today.

Saturday
February 5 *Tried lovemaking this morn. Satisfied him, but gave me more back pain.*
Evening was normal.

Sunday

February 6 *Jim is working this morning. Too much on my mind today. Went to Addison Airport Museum and had lunch at Bennigan's. He had 4 beers, I had 2 Margaritas. Very beautiful day.*

Monday

February 7 *Very good day at work, and a good evening at home.*

Tuesday

February 8 *Had my hair fixed this eve. Jim was NOT home when I got here. Came dragging in approx. 10:30 p.m. Said he had been drinking and parked at DART parking lot to "sleep it off."*

Wednesday

February 9 *Jim had been drinking again.*

Thursday

February 10 *Ice storm– I think he stayed home.*

Friday

February 11 *Jim had been drinking again.*

Saturday

February 12 *Went out with Jim today. Had a good time. Had dinner at Red Lobster.*

Sunday

February 13 *Went to lunch at Denny's on 35E, Red Oak–went shopping in Hillsboro. Came back to Red Bird Airport, then home. He became bored after dinner–wanted to go out. I wouldn't go: he*

went to Gold Rush–called me. I got dressed. Wrong thing to do.
When we got home, ready for bed, he INSISTED I turn my lamp off.
I wanted to talk to him, & tore lamp off the ceiling! And broke mom's
gift to me.

Monday
February 14 *Jim had been drinking again, and I'm so crushed over*
the damage he made last night.

Tuesday
February 15 *Jim had been drinking again, came to the beauty*
shop and made an ASS of himself as well as embarrassing me and
humiliating me in public as I was getting my hair cut. Bragging
about a Rolex watch (which he had in his pocket and probably had
been trying to sell it) he bought me for Valentine's Day, and I don't
like it!

Wednesday
February 16 *As always, he had been drinking again. Said he was*
leaving Texas. I had no response because I'm numb from all the
turmoil his drinking has caused. All I know is I have loved him with
all my heart and soul, and he just keeps wanting to hurt me with no
consideration for my feelings because he doesn't care. We went to
bed, and he never touched me.

Thursday
February 17 *I took ½ day vacation today. Jim came home early. We*
went to Red Bird Airport for Mexican dinner and a few drinks. Had
an enjoyable evening.

Friday
February 18 *Vacation day–not getting much accomplished. Jim working. Jim came home about 4:30 p.m.–had too much to drink. Insisted I go out to dinner with him–I said NO–he tried to leave twice, came back, looked at me angrily, and said go out with him so he wouldn't get in trouble. We went to Red Bird Airport for dinner & drinks: as always, in his state of mind, his "big mouth" was humiliating. I drove home.*

Saturday
February 19 *I asked him NOT to go to bars today (as he was leaving for work). I went to lunch alone at Red Bird. He had already been there drinking. He came in about 12:15 p.m. not knowing I was there. I left within 30 min. He came to the car, said I was embarrassing him to walk out. I went to Gold Rush for 1 hour and cried.*

Sunday
February 20 *Stayed at home, watched Olympics.*

Monday
February 21 *He reported to Probation Officer this morn., but when I was home for lunch, he had been drinking already. After I went back to work, he left again to go drinking. I blew up to him tonight. I have had enough of his stupidity.*

Tuesday
February 22 *He stayed home most of the day, but didn't drink. I got my hair set.*

Wednesday

February 23 *Jim worked today–didn't drink. We had a nice evening.*

Thursday

February 24 *Came home for lunch–mess in kitchen as usual. Jim came home within a few minutes: bought groceries & crab legs. He had been drinking already. Said he was going to stay home, fix salad & crab legs for dinner. I came home after work (garage door left open) he was NOT here, no salad fixed, & he had eaten all the crab legs. He came home 6:45 p.m., bought more crab legs, said a customer had called him & he went to meet with adjuster. BUT he had been out drinking more. Ugly evening–I was angry! No future in this kind of life.*

Friday

February 25 *Oh, Lord, what will this day bring? 6:15 a.m. I came home for lunch–garage door wide open! Jim had left the house approx. 8:30 a.m., & left it open. Nancy stopped in at office this morn. Said she had heard about J. R. hurting me. She is going to alert police to pick him up leaving one of the bars. She said I'm not strong enough to handle his drinking problem. He called me at work 4 p.m. & was very drunk. He left house again. Came home from work, he was not home. I went to Gold Rush for 2 hours. Came home 8 p.m., he was not home yet. I went to bed 10:00 p.m.*

Saturday

February 26 *Jim came home 7:05 a.m. Out all night. Said he slept in truck in a parking lot, N. Dallas. Bad day. I told him this eve, next time he goes drinking, come home first, pack clothes and Get Out! Jim Bryan called me today! I'm so happy.*

That last entry means that I called her. When Massey was acting this way I could speak to Mom as long as I wanted. This was as hard on me as it was on her.

Sunday
February 27 *Went shopping for groceries, watched TV, had nice dinner. Average day.*

Monday
March 7 *I took over doing deposits for 6 departments today. A busy day. Jim worked this morn.–soaking in the tub when I came home for lunch. He felt "punkish" and stayed home rest of day. Nice eve.*

Tuesday
March 8 *Jim has been gone all day–has not called. I came home after having hair set 6:10 p.m. Pouring down rain–he's not home yet. He came home 8:05 p.m. Had gone to N. Dallas to drink. Drank too much so he parked and slept it off. I was not a "Happy Camper."*

Wednesday
March 9 *Jack Steven called me at work this morn. He told me he's getting married Aug. 27. I'm so happy for him. Had the afternoon off (vacation time). Got my new driver's license. Called about Auto Ins. That was good news–less premium than ordinary Ins. Ha! Jim took me for my app't with Ass't D.A. I signed Affidavit dropping charges. We stopped at Red Bird Airport–saw Louis Wms. Then we went to Milano's for a great dinner. Came home exhausted after a great, great day. It has been so long since I felt this inner happiness.*

Thursday

March 10 *Jim got a speeding ticket & Inspection Sticker expired. So what else is new? More atty. fees. We went to Red Bird Airport after work. Came home about 7 p.m.–nice dinner, watched movie. Decent eve.*

Friday

March 11 *Jim took the day off: didn't answer phone stayed home, read books and watched TV. Pleasant evening.*

Saturday

March 12 *Went to Red Bird Airport. Nice day. Took a drive to Ovilla/ Glenn Heights to look at houses. Yuk!*

Sunday

March 13 *Went to Red Bird. Good day.*

Monday

March 14 *Jim has intestinal virus. Stayed home. Gene called me at work to see how I was doing.*

Tuesday

March 15 *Everything went "haywire" for me today. Was off $20.00 on City deposit (my fault in making change for Petty Cash box). Hem came out of my skirt at work. Ha! Jim still sick.*

Wednesday

March 16 *Jim still sick.*

Thursday

March 17 *Very pleasant birthday. They had cake and other goodies for me at work. Received several cards. Jack S. called me this eve. To wish a Happy Birthday. He and Susan are coming down this weekend. Jim still sick.*

Friday
March 18 *Had a good day at work. Jim is feeling better. We went to Red Bird. Brought home shrimp dinner.*

Saturday
March 19 *We took Jack & Susan to Red Bird Airport for Rib Eye diner. Had a great time. Jim got sick in the night. Stayed on couch all night.*

Sunday
March 20 *Jim still not feeling good.*

Monday
March 21 *Went to Dr. Gardner, Neurologist, at 3:15 p.m. today. I have a herniated disc in same area as the back surgery. Went back to office at 4:57 p.m. to tell Susan, Supervisor. When I left to go home, I cried, knowing how bad Jim had really hurt me and knowing what I have to go through now.*

Tuesday
March 22 *Went to Red Bird Airport tonight and had a great time dancing.*

Wednesday
March 23 *On vacation today. Went to Red Bird about noon. Laid around the house and rested remainder of day.*

Thursday
March 24 *Left for San Antonio about 10:30 a.m. Bluebonnets were beautiful. Got motel room about 4 p.m. Went to River Walk. Took a boat ride–had dinner at Mexican restaurant. Everything is beautiful.*

Friday
March 25 *Elegant breakfast buffet at the Marriott Hotel–went to IMAX theatre–went to the Alamo–took trolley car to Tower of the Americas (revolving restaurant). Went back to River Walk & had dinner at Rio Rio. Great food. Lovely day! Walked miles & miles. Ha!*

Saturday
March 26 *Had nice breakfast buffet at Hyatt hotel. Went to Sea World and headed for home. Had late lunch in New Braunsfel. Got home about 9 p.m.*

Sunday
March 27 *Lazy day–just rested. Jim bought 2 bottles Vodka in New Braunsfel yesterday and he drank too much today. I had a few.*

Monday
March 28 *Jim went to N. Dallas this afternoon to drink and play pool. Did not come home until 9 p.m. I'm so angry & upset. I don't need this. I hid remaining Vodka.*

Wednesday
March 30 *Went to Physical Therapist for treatment.*

Thursday
March 31 *Went to P.T. again for treatment. Supposed to start home exercises tonight, but too tired.*

Friday
April 1 *Worked hard at office today. Tried exercises, but was immediately interrupted when Jim wanted to start the laundry.*

Saturday
April 2 *Stayed home–tried to get relief for my back. Still painful. Rested today.*

Sunday
April 3 *Stayed home–just rested.*

Monday
April 4 *3rd treatment at Physical Therapist.*

Tuesday
April 5 *In bad pain most of day. Had my hair set.*

Wednesday
April 6 *Another painful day–4th treatment at P.T. Jim got the Auto Ins. Papers signed today.*

Thursday
April 7 *Feeling a little better today. Jim's intestinal infection is finally clearing up after a month. He finally got his bond handled for his speeding ticket.*

Friday

April 8 *Feeling O.K. today–very busy day at work. Susan (Supervisor) is on vacation today and all next week. Hope she comes back in a better frame of mind.*

Saturday

April 9 *Supposed to meet with CPA today–he has car trouble. Felt pretty good today.*

Sunday

April 10 *Miserable this morn. A lot of pain.....*

Tuesday

April 12 *Pain*

Wednesday

April 13 *Pain*

Thursday

April 14 *Pain*

Friday

April 15 *Pain*

Saturday

April 16 *Went to Cedar Hill to look at Garden Homes. Pain*

Sunday

April 17 *Talked to Jack today. Mathew is living with his mom.*

Monday
April 18 *Pain*

Tuesday
April 19 *Called Neurologist to see what next step is. He ordered MRI. Pain*

Wednesday
April 20 *Pain*

Thursday
April 21 *Pain. Had MRI this afternoon.*

Friday
April 22 *Vacation today. Feeling somewhat better. Jim was sick all day. Intestinal problem flared up again. Went to drug store to get him medicine for his watery, itchy eyes.*

Saturday
April 23 *Feeling pretty good. Ran errands. Jim is better today.*

Sunday
April 24 *Jim left to get truck washed. Gone for 40 min. Went out for breakfast (he said) then changed his mind. Did not get truck washed. We went shopping at Mall. I bought purse & black skirt.*

Monday
April 25 *Tornado hit Lancaster & DeSoto. Bad damage. Jim went out to breakfast. (The "sort of" unexplained 20-25 miles on the truck*

again.) He has been acting so strange for about 6 wks. Soaks in tub 1 to 2 hrs. every day, sometimes twice a day. Seems to "live" in the bathroom.

Tuesday
April 26 *He went to Lancaster & Kennedale to observe damage.*

Wednesday
April 27 *Feeling a little better.*

Thursday
April 28 *Feeling a little better.*

Friday
April 29 *Went to Red Bird Airport, and over to Milano's for Italian Dinner.*

Saturday
April 30 *Bad pain today.*

Sunday
May 1 *Bad pain, but went to grocery store by myself. Jim sick with diarrhea.*

Monday
May 2 *Got results on MRI test. Bulging #3 disc. He suggested steroid injections. I will not do that.*

Tuesday
May 3 *Called P. Therapist. He said more therapy could help.*

Wednesday
May 4 *I called Dr. George, chiropractor. Had 1st treatment this eve. Made me feel better. Did 1 exercise he showed me, 10 times.*

Thursday
May 5 *Did exercise 15 times. Feeling fair. Always morning pain bad.*

Friday
May 6 *Went to Dr. George, 2nd treatment. We went to Red Bird Airport tonight. Jim was sick all night–diarrhea.*

Saturday
May 7 *He was still in bathroom 6 a.m. I voted and ran errands. Felt bad pain all afternoon.*

Sunday
May 8 *Was up 4:30 a.m.–suffering bad. Will this never end?!!*

Friday
May 13 *Went to Red Bird.*

Friday
May 20 *Last day at work for 10 days. Went to Red Bird.*

Saturday
May 21 *I worked 6 1/2 hours today. Went to Red Bird–got groceries.*

Sunday
May 22 *Went to Red Bird–I got drunk. Became angry after I got home. Jim left once again for N. Dallas. I locked him out. He got in*

through patio door.
Monday
May 23 *Spent most of day in bed–Jim ate all day–as usual, never
cleaned up anything. I HATE IT!!*
 Some vacation!

Tuesday
May 24 *Going to Dr. again. Jim left 8:30 a.m. to return movies and
who knows what else.*

This was the last entry made. She included some letters written
directly to Massey. God only knows if he read them.

Chapter Eight

Turn Me Loose

IN EARLY 1995, MOM SPOKE with Trisha on the phone quite a bit. Trisha had just turned fifteen on the tenth of January. I guess Mom really wanted to open up to her. They talked about troubles the two of them were having in their relationships. Trisha had chosen the worst kid in the ninth grade as her boyfriend. This young man's family tolerated his highly outrageous behavior because he was the star. He could do anything athletic. Trisha was a handful all by herself, so every time the two were together, it was like World War III. Mom had been through the ringer and back during her short marriage to Massey, so there was a sort of bond, but it's sad to call it that.

Mom would turn sixty in March. All of us really wanted her to come spend her birthday at our house. It was never said, but she knew not to bring her husband. We all were pretty excited about the whole idea, so we planned a great big party. My brother had met and married a nice girl, Susan, so our party guest list included: Jack, Susan, Sheri and I, the kids, and Mom. We celebrated into the night with old stories, some embarrassing pictures from our childhood, plenty of food, and laughs. I used up an entire roll of film that night. Mom really felt good. She was overdue to blow off some steam. Mom's birthday get-together had little to do with the gifts that were given; it was more about us reconnecting. That was the seventeenth of March.

My career had grown to route supervisor, which meant that when I had an assigned operator off for vacation, I had to fill in to run the weekly linen pick-up and deliveries. James, a route man who worked for me, was well-deserving of his one-week vacation. I had ridden with him enough to know that his customers really liked him. The majority of his stops appreciated some of the little extras he had done to retain their business. Truck keys in hand, I was ready for that Monday morning.

You tend to find out over your life that someone beating on your door late at night or early in the morning is never good. Somewhere between 3:00 and 4:00 a.m., on the tenth of April, Officer Frazier, from the Iowa Park Police Department, pounded on our front door. Startled, as you can expect, I jumped out of bed, with Sheri right behind me. My heart was thumping by the time I reached for the light switch. Once I had the front porch light glowing, we peaked through the blinds to check out the person rattling our house at such an early hour. The uniform calmed and scared me at the same time.

We both knew the kids were home safe and sound and that neither of us had ever done anything to warrant a visit from our local law enforcement. My mind raced with all the scenarios that would give the authorities any reason for an early-morning visit. As my blood pressure spiked, we let the policeman in the house.

He told us the police in Duncanville knew Mom had a son who lived in Iowa Park. A Duncanville officer had phoned the Iowa Park office to have a patrolman sent to our house. The message was only to have me call the Duncanville police as soon as I could. Officer Frazier had the number to the police station. I grabbed the phone right away and dialed. As I waited for them to answer, I had the overwhelming sensation that we were going to be told Mom was dead. Andy, from the Duncanville detectives division, answered. I told him who I was.

"Mr. Pulley," he said, "I'm afraid I have some bad news. Your mother is dead."

I collapsed and cried for a minute.

When you hear that you've lost a parent, it's like the wind is instantly sucked out of your body. All of my joints went limp. Thoughts were flashing in my mind at the speed of light. Mental pictures, assumptions, regrets, laughter, tears, fights, and feelings rushed to my brain. I was momentarily in "information overload". All of this data had clogged any clear thinking.

I took a long, deep breath. After composing myself, I asked what had happened. Knowing now what I did not know then, I can imagine Detective Andy really didn't want me to ask, but I'm sure he was prepared. It's always best to tell it straight. Once I asked Andy the question, he never hesitated.

He responded in a kind but firm voice, "Your mother was shot last night."

"That son of a bitch shot my mom!" My voice was so loud I woke up the kids.

Andy waited on the phone until my wailing had died to a blubbering, sniffling sobbing and he asked, "Mr. Pulley, who do you think shot your mother?"

"James Reginald Massey," my voice quivered, full of anger.

Andy asked what made me think he had done it. I explained some things, but I'm sure they had enough details of his past that he was their only suspect. I told Andy it would take at least three hours, but we would be there to take care of as much of this as we could.

I knew I had to move as quickly as possible. I had a route that needed attending, so I couldn't just pick up and leave. The first call I made was to my supervisor. Harvey was a little guy who I'd known for about eleven years; he was no spring chicken. I was convinced, no matter what the circumstance, that there was no way he would agree to drive this route.

In the middle of hearing the gut-wrenching news of Mom's murder, I now had the added burden of finding a qualified operator for a five-day linen route. Sheri and I quickly packed a few things. Trisha didn't hesitate to throw some clothes in a bag so she could come with us. We told Tyler to carry on until we had a chance to come get him later in the week. God blessed us with good children, and Tyler was about as good as they come. We also had our oldest son, Todd, living close by. We knew he and Tyler could come to Duncanville in a couple of days.

The chance that my regular route guy, James, would be at home with no plans for his vacation was pretty strong. James was, and still is, a down-to-earth, hard-working fellow. I have considered him a friend for many years. The sun was just beginning to come up when we drove up to James's house. Overcast skies produced one of those light, misting rains that morning. The chill in the air caused a little fog on my glasses as I banged on his door. Thoughts of Officer Frazier rattling the front of our house swirled while I waited in the chilly dampness. James cautiously opened his door. To this day, I can still see his reaction when I tearfully explained my reality. As I had suspected, he had no plans for his week off. Without flinching, he grabbed the keys to the truck from my hand. His voice was reassuring as he told me not to worry and go on. I gave him a tearful hug of gratitude. My memory is a little spotty, but I do remember running to the car without looking back.

The girls and I arrived at the Duncanville, Texas, police station early on April 10, 1995. Everyone became focused on finding all of the answers to this horrific crime as soon as legally possible. The vision is crystal clear of sitting in Jim Cowsert's office. His face was stern, but we all felt how kind and concerned he was. One of the first questions I asked after we had arrived was, "Where is she?" I couldn't come to grips with the fact that she was gone. He walked us through some of the details his partners had uncovered from their brief investigative work.

Unbelievably, it had only been a few hours since her death. They were careful not to interrupt any crime-scene evidence from the night before. You see, this crime came on the heals of the infamous O. J. Simpson case where, if you recall, the Los Angeles police as well as their detectives had been accused of sloppy work. Mom was one of the city's own, having been employed there for over ten years. She was the one who handled payday. Naturally, everyone knew Pat. All of Mom's fellow employees at the City of Duncanville liked her and, above all, trusted her. We could see that those who knew her took this case very personally.

Most employees had either witnessed Massey coming into the office with his big mouth moving, or they had heard some of the horror stories from their coworkers. This was the guy who had been booked into the city jail for petty theft at a local Tom Thumb grocery store and for a DWI. Who knows what other stunts his alcohol-soaked mind led him to do? The clues, evidence, and gut reaction all pointed to Mom's husband of just over four years as the prime suspect.

Monday was spent making arrangements for a one-week stay and a funeral. We had family in seven states to get in touch with. Our close family network eliminated the need for me to make a dozen calls. Mom's sister Carolyn was the first person I got in touch with. My brother and I had spoken earlier that morning, which meant my immediate family was as informed as could be. Realizing that we would need several rooms, we reserved an entire block at a local hotel. Keeping an open line of communication was critical at this point. Sheri and I had to spend a lot of time in the hotel by the phone. Cell phones were not something everyone owned or had any access to. We needed more information, and most of all, the family wanted James R. Massey in jail.

After a restless night, we went to the funeral home to pick out a casket. Jack and Susan had arrived late Monday. Several difficult decisions had to be made, and none of these mind-numbing choices could have been made without him. For whatever reason, Jack and I found ourselves alone for a few minutes. All of my emotions had balled up inside me. Once Jack and I were isolated in the showroom, something internally blew. We had been slapped with a full dose of the harshness this kind of shock can deliver. Every muscle had gone limp like a rubber band. My bubble burst. I cried so hard that I nearly lost my balance.

Life is funny, how it seems to run in cycles. When you are very young, you really don't remember much. All you know is what you're told.

Once you start school, you are away from your parents for most of the day. Your family depends on a teacher to become mentor and babysitter. The realization is that you only have a few people you can truly depend on. One thing most people miss is that person should be you. I am a slow learner, so I felt early on that my big brother was the one. That deep-seeded trust is still etched inside. Age-wise, Jack and I are only two and a half years apart. We rode the school bus together, played army, fought, hung out, and had some very good times. I think it was that life lesson that crept back into my distorted thought process on the morning we picked out our mother's final resting place.

Funeral directors walk a fine line during these moments. They become soft-spoken, trustworthy, comforting salespeople. Since death is permanent, there is little chance of repeat business. "I'm sure you'd want the best for your mother," is the funeral director's phrase of choice. There are so many extras a family can put into arranging a full-blown sendoff for a loved one. Given our circumstance, the barrage of questions from the sales department became a little overwhelming. Clearly, there was no need for a concrete encasement around the casket.

We had spent an agonizing hour or two with the funeral home staff. Now came time to visit the cemetery. There was absolutely no way we were going to bury our mom with someone else's last name on her headstone. The cemetery never questioned the use of our last name even though Mom's legal name was, painfully, Massey.

You will find my parents lying side-by-side beneath towering oak trees. Little Bethel Cemetery has them permanently listed as Jack C. and Patricia L. Pulley. This became one of the few peaceful moments for our family during the week of Mom's funeral.

73

The rest of the day was spent between the police station and visiting with some of the friends Mom had made at work. We met with the chaplain of the fire department and shared some stories. We also met with the city manager and the entire staff Mom was surrounded by every day she worked. I can still see the red rose someone had laid on her desk. It caught my attention when we first walked in. There were several times when I was overcome with the shock of what had happened. The result was getting completely choked up. Seeing the rose on her desk meant, to me, that she was loved and well-thought-of as a coworker.

While all of the arrangements were being made, I asked the officials at the fire department as well as the police force if they would choose three representatives from each agency to serve as pallbearers for Mom. Without hesitation we had the six needed positions filled, which was even more testament to the impression Mom had made. Warm feelings surround my thoughts toward everyone who was involved. This heartfelt emotion goes out to the investigators of the crime as well as the folks who stood out and made a difference in our lives that week.

With most crimes, there is an autopsy, and then the body is sent to the funeral home. This process takes some time; however, we finally got to see Mom on Tuesday night. The dimly lit viewing room was quiet and creepy. The vivid memory from the first time I saw her that evening will remain in my mind forever. My mother was a very attractive lady. We had located Mom's regular hairdresser, who had volunteered to fix her hair like she always wore it. She was wearing a flowing, light green dress. She did not appear to be sixty years old. Funny—that is what the coroner's report stated.

Slowly bending over the casket, I kissed her. My body was numb from the firestorm of anger, hatred, disbelief, and pure loss of a loved one. Placing your lips on a lifeless body is more of a natural reaction than a sensible act. I believe, once you've passed away, your soul moves on to Heaven. The body is just God's way to help you get around.

It's rare that you ever know the impression you leave on people. Tuesday night Sheri and I were shocked and relieved to see our very best friends show up at the hotel. Gary and Jean were our traveling buddies as well as our overall closest friends. Gary was a jovial fellow. He had been through divorce more than once. Jean was a classy lady, a single parent who grew tired of being lonely. She and Gary had truly discovered a unique, loving companionship. Both of them sacrificed vacation days to come to Duncanville to be with us. They were there simply to do whatever was needed. Friendship like ours is a once-in-a-lifetime relationship. Sheri and I had been thrown overboard without a life preserver, and we were growing tired of treading water. Gary and Jean had come to our rescue. Before the week was over, Gary would make two more trips to Wichita Falls, shuttling our kids and taking care of various problems.

Mom's sisters and brother had loaded up in a couple of vehicles to drive in from Indiana. As they drove the one thousand miles, we spoke to them a few times on Jeanne's shoebox-size cell phone. We were expecting them in on Wednesday, April 12. Early that day, our hotel room phone rang. The Duncanville police had arrested Massey. Not long after getting the news, Aunt Carolyn called to check in. Their caravan erupted in cheers when I relayed the latest news to our family. We truly thought our pain and suffering from his act of senseless violence would have closure now that he was incarcerated.

For whatever reason, Jack was running late and seemed to be finding reasons to not rush down to the city jail with me to watch Massey being booked into the facility. My emotions, thoughts, and hopes were running at light speed. I was so geared up to stand outside just to stare him down, as if to say, "We got you now." This became one of those moments that I should have taken matters into my own hands. I still don't understand what was holding my brother back, but he dragged his feet so long that the police had Massey booked and in the cell before we got to the jail.

Of course, I had no desire to pay him a visit, but there was a request from Massey. When the police found him, he was staying in a flea-bag hotel, which had a bar, of course. The detectives dragged him out of his room without taking any of his personal belongings. There is still no explanation of how he fell and suffered those bruises and cuts, but as we all know, he did drink heavily. Massey needed some of his underwear, T-shirts, and socks from the house. He asked the police to call me for permission to enter Mom's residence to gather some clothing. I gave the police permission to enter the house.

Our legal system, such that it is, states that a person is presumed innocent until a fair trial proves his or her guilt. There was never a doubt in any of our minds that James Massey had pulled the trigger on the single-shot .22-caliber handgun, sending a bullet through Mom's right cheek on that Sunday night.

We spent a lot more time at the hotel with the arrival of our family. Jack and I made numerous trips to Dallas-Fort Worth airport. Without volunteering, I was becoming the go-to guy. My small, black notebook filled up rapidly with all of our contacts, business cards, direct numbers, addresses, names of people I had spoken with, and every bit of pertinent information I felt would be of some use.

Making sure our family was taken care of was bittersweet in the sense that we were spending time together in the hotel, plus sharing our grief. Not much of a reunion, but it sure looked like it inside of the hospitality room at the Holiday Inn. As a family, we have always laughed and enjoyed each other's company. This gathering had a small piece of that. Even in the middle of a tragic situation, there is a need to cut up and relish time with family. It relieved our thoughts of all the unrealistic onslaught of a sudden murder, a suspect on the loose, Mom in the morgue, and the police without the weapon. Healthy distractions became part of the process to retain our sanity.

God will truly only give you as much as He thinks you can handle. Our minds will shut out the grim and let in the lightheartedness of a good laugh or a warm, friendly hug to keep us focused. My undivided attention had to be on setting up a respectable final service for Mother. I had a few ideas of what to do with her personal effects, but that would have to wait until later.

Soon after I went to bed the night before the funeral, our phone rang twice. The first call came from Tennessee. It wasn't family, even though the caller had specifically asked for me. I got on the phone. Our room was pitch-dark, and my wife was close by to see who was calling from Chattanooga. It was, to our surprise, Massey's first wife, Becky. She was a very polite, soft-spoken lady. Her first words were sympathetic toward our loss. I think she was driven to call due to the fact that, while married to Massey, he had never been physically abusive. The thought of his ability to pull a gun and use it baffled her. She went on to explain that during their marriage, he had built a landscaping business in Florida. Massey had gotten himself into cocaine use and literally lost everything by shooting the drug into his veins. She commented that since they had two daughters, there was no way she could continue to live that lifestyle. It forced her to leave. After divorcing his wife, Massey moved to California to live with his mommy.

The second call came not long after the first. This one was from Massey's youngest daughter. Becky had told me that Jamie was the only child who would speak to him. From what I understand, the older of the two had disowned him and adamantly refused to reconcile their differences. Jamie was the daughter we had met a couple of years earlier, when she had shown up at Mom's house with the new grandbaby. She was the young lady who couldn't believe her dad was acting so foolish and asked me, "Is he always this way?" Her purpose for calling was to find out if I thought he had actually done it.

I did not hesitate to answer. "Of course he did it." I detailed some of the physically abusive punishment he had put Mom through over the short time they were married. Jamie still didn't believe it, so I left it at that. Considering the entire situation was so bizarre, I tried to keep a calm head. I had to get off the phone and get some rest. Changing the subject, I asked Massey's daughter how her baby was doing.

She hesitated, then answered, "She is fine. Thank you for asking." She said she was sorry for calling so late. Thankfully, that was the end of it.

After a few tosses and turns, I was able to fall asleep. Thinking of putting a loved one in the ground has an uneasy finality about it. Trying to make any sense of what we were experiencing was beginning to take its toll. Everything from arranging a funeral to taking calls from my little boss, who wanted me back at work, was wearing me down. I was exhausted.

Thursday, April 13, 1995, came along like any other day for most people. All around us, I could imagine people hustling kids off to school or grabbing something to eat on their way out the door. Our family awoke to a strange place, the Holiday Inn in Duncanville, Texas. The hotel had become our home base during the past few days. Most of our time had been spent in the funeral home, city hall, Mom's house, or the police station. The whole thing seems like a confusing blur without much clarity.

Words are very hard to come by when I try describing that morning. My wife Sheri and I were blessed to have our children there. They were, and are still, supportive, loving individuals. Todd was twenty, Trisha had just turned fifteen, and Tyler was thirteen. They all looked very nice for the service. It wasn't a drawn-out affair. The chaplain said some very nice things, read some scripture, then ended with a prayer. During his service, he attempted to help us through a trying moment. There, in the chapel, lay our mother's body in a beautiful casket, with a tiny bullet hole in her right cheek. Her wound was not visible, but everyone knew it was there. Yes, I know Jack and I wanted the best for our mother. Without reservation I can say we were successful in our attempt to deliver.

After we had filed past the coffin to view her body for the very last time, I made a point of approaching the six pallbearers. Fighting through my tears, I shook every one of their hands as I thanked them. That seemed like the thing to do at the time. After all, they had known Mom and worked with her every day. It wasn't easy for them to perform such a duty. The three firefighters and three police officers responded quickly to our request. For their service, I will be forever grateful.

I've ridden to three graveyards in the back of a long limousine. The first time was for my best friend. He was only seventeen when he was killed. I was just sixteen. The second was Dad's funeral. I distinctly remember that day. This time was different, for all the wrong reasons. I cannot picture our family's ride to Little Bethel Cemetery. One pleasant memory was the number of people who came to the gravesite. Obviously it showed the impact Mom had made on their lives. She could do that to people. She had a way of reading a person and understanding their personality. She had a way of making you feel good. My mom had a big smile and hardy laugh to go along with all of it. We will never know why she accepted such a disturbed individual into her world.

The night of the thirteenth was somber. We all retreated to the hospitality room. Our family made the most of our last night together, knowing Mom would have wanted it that way. Anger was the main theme that evening, but when our family unites, there is always a sprinkling of humor. There is something about a good laugh that warms a person all over. I had cried so much over the past few days that my tank had just about dried up. Having all of Mom's loved ones in one room was priceless. The night was short, because they all had a long drive home, and most were leaving first thing the next morning. After making sure everyone was safe and sound in their rooms, I remember holding Sheri close in bed. She is and always has been a good, loving wife.

Friday the fourteenth held no surprises for any of us. We were all determined to have Mom's house emptied before leaving town. Only after entering the 1,900-square-foot home did I realize what a daunting task we had ahead of us. I had a wealth of willing volunteers.

My approach was to use a team of people in every room. Starting in the kitchen, I instructed Tyler and Trisha to start boxing up all of the dishes, pots, pans, and silverware. Our friends, Jean and Gary, began filling boxes in the master bath and bedroom. Cousin Pam was given the guest bedroom. She understood the importance of saving family photos. Mom kept them stored in the guest closet.

My next move was to get all of the furniture moved into the front yard. We had made an appointment with a battered and abused women's organization to come pick up all of the household goods. Everything was running like a well-oiled machine. No one was standing or waiting for something to do. Abruptly, Jack put a cog in the wheel. He erupted with a loud request for everyone to *stop*. He had some issues with the decision I made to give everything away. Mom's furniture was in good shape, but she had had it for several years. Needing some closure, we didn't have the time or energy to sell it. Giving it to a worthy organization would put it to better use. She had everything to furnish a couple of small homes, which would have assisted the shelter.

Jack was getting started with a new family. He and Susan had been married only since September. His personal belongings were in need of an upgrade. He made it clear, in his own special way, that he needed a few things. Point-blank, I told him to go get a U-Haul truck. The number of people we had working would make it easy to help him load it up. Right after Jack left, our oldest son mentioned his need for a couch and dining table. Without missing a beat, we put all of the items aside for Jack and Todd, then continued our emptying of the house. Jack came back with a truck in a surprisingly short amount of time. We all loaded his fridge, piano, two couches, and the recliner. Everything in boxes went to the front yard and by 3:00 p.m., our voices echoed in the house. There was no way James Massey was getting back in the house.

I made a point of changing the locks on the front and back doors. We pushed the truck out of the garage into the driveway. Pulling the release on the overhead door would prevent anyone from getting in through the garage. All of the junk Massey called his own wound up in the bed of the little pickup Mom had purchased for him. Somehow all of the leftover food from the refrigerator found its way into the back of the truck, too. I realize our actions sound childish, but it seemed like a good idea at the time.

We made sure the hot water heater was off but left the cold water to the house on. With the last bit of energy drained out of my system, I found the strength to double-check that all the lights were off and doors locked. My parents had only lived there four years. Good memories had been forged in such a short period. Precious time spent with family had all been marred by a rapid chain of horrendous events.

The ride home was longer than usual. It seemed as though we had accomplished a lot, but we all still felt very empty and confused. Our family had a little experience with the legal system, but not at this level. The Duncanville police detectives assured us that every resource would be made available. We were all certain that we had the person who had committed the crime. All the employees of the city were behind us and wished us well. The healing process should have begun or at least started to take root; however, nothing could have prepared any of us for what was coming.

Chapter Nine

Throw Away the Key

E VER PLAYED THE GAME OF STARTING a story with one person then whispering what you heard into the next person's ear? Once it gets around to the last one in line, the details can change. Police reports work a little bit like that. I have read the R.O.'s (or reporting officer's) reports from the night of Mom's murder. Some of the numerous accounts are basic, and others are very detailed. The emotionally difficult process of taking in those facts from an unbiased report of the crime scene at Mom's house has taken its toll. Memories of events that took place over the years Mom was married to this viciously abusive criminal are still very clear in my mind. I wasn't there the night he took her life. Taking careful aim toward accuracy, I have selected the following statements. The police officers, detectives, EMTs, and all other official personnel have painted the picture. The Freedom of Information Act allows us all to review exactly what took place. One of the first patrol officers on the scene was Officer Moon.

DUNCANVILLE POLICE DEPARTMENT-
Offense/Incident Report
D Moon #117

On 04-09-1995 at approx 9:29 pm R/O was dispatched to a shooting call at an unknown address next door to 211 Hillcroft. R/O was informed by dispatch, while enroute to the location, that a male subject might be at the location armed with an unknown type weapon.

When R/O arrived at the location, Ofc. Holcomb was exiting his vehicle and approaching the front of 211 Hillcroft. R/O observed there was a white female standing on the front porch of 211 Hillcroft, a white male in a white t-shirt and shorts, and a white male subject in a red long sleeved shirt and dark colored pants were in the front yard area between the addresses of 211 Hillcroft and 215 Hillcroft. R/O observed the white male subject in white t-shirt and shorts was standing in the yard area and the white male subject in the red long sleeved shirt and dark colored pants was kneeling near a tree in the front yard of 215 Hillcroft.

Ofc. Holcomb and R/O visually observed that none of the subjects appeared to be armed with a weapon. Ofc. Holcomb and R/O contacted the white male subject in the red long sleeved shirt and dark colored pants, later identified as Massey, James Reginald w/m, and he advised his wife, later identified as Massey, Pat w/f, was inside the residence at 215 Hillcroft and needed help.

R/O observed that Massey appeared to be very upset and

frantic. Ofc. Holcomb advised Massey, James to remain outside the residence and the subject became very upset and attempted to enter the residence at 215 Hillcroft. Ofc. Holcomb and R/O again told Massey, James to remain outside the residence and he complied. R/O observed the front door of the residence appeared to be closed and the front porch light was off. Ofc. Holcomb opened the front door of the residence, which was unlocked and entered followed by R/O.

Ofc. Holcomb entered the living room of the location and walked towards the hallway which led off from the east side of the living room. R/O entered the residence living room and Ofc. Holcomb entered the hallway leading from the east side of the living room. Ofc. Holcomb walked north down the hallway which led to a bedroom located at the northeast corner of the residence. R/O entered the hallway and followed Ofc. Holcomb towards the bedroom.

R/O reached the open door to the northeast bedroom and observed a white female subject, later identified as Massey, Pat w/f, who was laying on the floor on the west side of the bedroom. R/O observed that the Massey, Pat subject was lying on her back with what appeared to be a small wound on her right cheek and blood appeared to have run from her nose. R/O observed there was a large area of blood on the carpet beneath her head. R/O observed the subject's right arm was lifted up over her head and there was a ring on one of the fingers of her right hand. Ofc. Holcomb remained in the bedroom and R/O walked back down the hallway, through the living room, and exited the open front door of the residence.

R/O contacted Massey, James who was kneeling next to a tree located in the southwest part of the front yard. R/O observed the subject was still very upset, frantic, and crying. R/O asked the subject if there were any weapons inside the residence and he advised there was a .38-caliber handgun located in the closet of the master bedroom of the location, where the Massey, Pat subject was found. R/O inquired as to the subject's identity and obtained a TX Picture Dl #xxxxxxxx which the subject removed from his wallet.

R/O asked the subject what had occurred and he advised that he and his wife, Massey, Pat had went to Redbird Airport between 3 & 4 pm on this date and had several drinks each. R/O could smell the strong odor of an alcoholic beverage on or about the breath of the subject. He advised they left together at an unknown time and went to Cutters, at an unknown location. He advised they both had (1) one drink at the location. He advised they left Cutters together and went to the residence at 215 Hillcroft.

He advised that after they entered the residence Massey, Pat began to get upset in reference to her deceased husband, which he advised she always does when she drinks. He advised he left the location, which he always does when she gets upset after drinking. He advised that at no time did they get into an argument or disturbance at the residence. He advised he drove down 67 to Collins, turned around, and drove back to Hampton. He advised he went up Hampton and back to Redbird. At that point he became very upset, crying, and demanding to go into the residence to see Massey, Pat.

He repeatedly stated to R/O, "She's dead isn't she?" He advised R/O he had driven back to the residence after leaving Redbird and entered the residence from the rear. He advised he entered the living room and hollered "Pat." He advised she did not answer and that he called for her (3) three or (4) four more times and she didn't answer. He advised he observed that the light was on in the northeast bedroom of the residence and entered that bedroom. He advised he found Massey, Pat on the bedroom floor with blood on her face. He advised he checked for a pulse on her neck and did not feel one. He advised he also observed that she was not breathing.

He advised that he then left the location. At that time, he began crying and trying to enter the residence to see about Massey, Pat. R/O observed that Massey, James had a red substance, which appeared to be blood, on the middle finger of his right hand. R/O stayed with Massey, James outside the residence while the paramedics removed Massey, Pat from the residence and placed her into ambulance #792 which was manned by paramedics Steve Hamm and John Clark.

R/O was asked by one of the paramedics to get Massey, James away from the ambulance because he was attempting to enter the rear of the ambulance. R/O retrieved his marked squad car which was parked approx (3) three houses west of 215 Hillcroft and pulled behind ambulance #792. R/O advised he would escort Massey, James to the hospital when Massey, Pat was transported. Massey, James agreed and sat down in the front seat of the squad car.

R/O transported Massey, James to Charlton Methodist Hospital where ambulance #792 transported Massey, Pat. R/O escorted Massey, James into the hospital and stayed in his presence constantly at the hospital. R/O observed that Massey, James did not make any phone calls from the hospital and repeatedly went from being calm to being very upset and demanding to see Massey, Pat.

R/O observed upon arrival at Charlton Methodist Hospital that Massey, James had several small wet areas on the front of the right side of his shirt. R/O was contacted by Inv. Ainley at the hospital and R/O informed him of what he had observed at the residence and what Massey, James had said. R/O was in a private visitor room at the hospital with Massey, James, Inv. Ainley, and (2) two hospital security guards when the doctor informed Massey, James that Massey, Pat was deceased and explained to him the bullet wound injury she had received. R/O observed Massey, James became very upset and began to cry.

R.O was advised by Inv. Ainley to escort Inv. McDaniel along with Massey, James back to the residence at 215 Hillcroft in Inv. McDaniel's unmarked squad car. R/O road back to the location with them and left his marked squad car at the hospital.

After arriving at the residence, R/O began writing his report while seated in a marked squad car outside the front of the residence. R/O was contacted by Sgt. Cowsert and advised to escort Massey, James to a private residence located at 219 Hillcroft where he could use the restroom. R/O was informed to not allow Massey, James to wash his hands or get them wet. R/O observed that Massey, James did not wash his hands in the restroom and was escorted back outside to the roadway in front of 215 Hillcroft where he was in the presence of Inv. McDaniel.

I never personally met Officer Moon; however, his report speaks volumes about his professionalism. His attention to detail is evident. This report supports the fact that officers see things that most of us don't want to think about. We can only assume what this officer of the law was thinking. Most reports refrain from personal feelings.

Affidavit for arrest warrant or capias:
Report by Officer G. McDaniel

On 04/09/1995, at approximately 9:29 p.m. Officer L. Holcomb #104 and Officer D. Moon #117, of the Duncanville Police Department, responded to a shooting call at 215 Hillcroft Drive, Duncanville, Dallas County, Texas. Upon arrival, Officer Holcomb observed the Defendant, Massey, James Reginald W/M, 10/06/42, hereafter referred to as the Defendant, kneeling in the front of 215 Hillcroft Drive, sobbing. The Defendant then stated to Officer Holcomb #104, "She's been shot!"

Officers Holcomb and Moon, then entered the residence of 215 Hillcroft Drive, Duncanville, Texas. Officer Holcomb arrived in the master bedroom of this residence and observed Patricia Pulley Massey, W/F 03/17/35, age 60, Texas driver's license XXXXXXXX hereafter referred to as the deceased, laying on her back, lifeless, with blood coming from her nose and mouth. Officer Holcomb notified Police communications immediately to dispatch an ambulance. Duncanville Paramedics responded and transported the deceased to Charlton Methodist Hospital.

At approximately 10:15 p.m. the deceased was pronounced dead by Dr. Tsou. The deceased arrived at the hospital at 10:03 p.m., Emergency Room personnel began treatment immediately, by approximately 10:13 p.m. Dr. Tsou stated that he could not find an entry wound, just a fracture on the back of the skull. At approximately 10:17 p.m. Dr. Tsou stated that the skull was definitely cracked, but there was still no point of entry to indicate a gunshot wound. The gun shot entry wound was not found until 10:37 p.m., after Dr. Tsou ordered X-rays and the deceased was cleaned. Investigator A. Ainley #069, of the Duncaville Police Department, was present during the examination of the deceased by Emergency Room personnel and Dr. Tsou.

Investigator Ainley interviewed the defendant regarding the whereabouts of the deceased and the defendant prior to the reporting of the incident to Police. The defendant stated, he and the deceased had been to a bar and restaurant from 3:00 p.m. until 5:00 p.m. The defendant then stated that the deceased became very upset after they had arrived home to 215 Hillcroft Drive. The defendant then left the residence to drive around, leaving the deceased at home. The defendant returned to the residence of 215 Hillcroft Drive to find his wife dead. During this interview the defendant stated he only had a ".38" and a 30-30 rifle. A Search Warrant was obtained for 215 Hillcroft Drive, Duncanville, Dallas County, Texas on 04/10/95, signed by Dallas County, District Judge, Larry W. Baraka at 2:15 a.m. The Search Warrant was necessary based on the defendant's original refusal of a consensual search.

Investigator G. McDaniel #068 of the Duncanville Police Department and M. Courtney, T. Ekis, and J. Brooks, of Forensic Consultant Services conducted a search of the residence. This search revealed the following items: .38 cal. Handgun, .25 cal. Handgun, 30-30 cal. Rifle and a .16 gauge shotgun. Assorted rounds of ammunition were also found, in particular an opened box of .22 cal. Cartridges, sitting on a shelf in the closet of the master bedroom. Three additional rounds of .22 cal. Cartridges were found beneath this box on the closet floor. No .22 cal. Weapon(s) were found in or around the residence. An analog, electric alarm clock was found next to the area where the deceased was found with the time stopped at 7:59 p.m. No forced entry into the residence was found.

On 04/11/95, Investigators A. Sims #084 and G. McDaniel #068 of the Duncanville Police Department, obtained a written statement from Ronald D. Carroll, the employer of the defendant who stated the following, Mr. Carroll received a telephone call on 4/11/95 at approximately 7:40 p.m. from the defendant. The defendant stated that he and the deceased started arguing and the deceased told him to leave. The defendant refused and according to the defendant, the deceased got his gun from under the bed and he wrestled her for it and the gun went off. In this same written statement by Mr. Carroll, he (Mr. Carroll), indicated that in the past he had personally spoke to the deceased and she told him of the defendant being drunk, mad and chasing her around the house with a gun telling her that he would "KILL" her if she left him. Mr. Carroll also wrote that the deceased indicated to him that plans had been made to leave the defendant.

In a verbal statement by Nancy Ramsey to Investigator Ainley, Ms. Ramsey stated that she had personal conversations with the deceased in the past regarding the defendant's drinking and abusive behavior. During these conversations with the deceased Ms. Ramsey would ask why the deceased would not leave the defendant and the deceased replied, that the defendant had told her that "no matter where I go, he will KILL me!"

Investigator Sims was present during the autopsy, performed by Dr. Guileyardo of the Dallas County Medical Examiners Office. At 9:24 a.m. recovered a .22 cal. Bullet from head of deceased.

Investigator McDaniel obtained a written statement on 4/11/95 from Mr. Gary Poplin, who knows the defendant and spoke to him at a bar during the time frame of Thanksgiving and Christmas of 1994. Mr. Poplin and the defendant's conversation were regarding a .22 cal. Handgun the defendant said he owned.

Due to inconsistent statements made by the defendant, the weapon missing from the crime scene, the threats made to the deceased by the defendant, and the defendant's early outcry that his wife had been shot when it took trauma medical professionals approximately 30 minutes to determine that the deceased had been shot, therefore your Affiant believes that the defendant, James Reginald Massey did intentionally and knowingly cause the death of Patricia Pulley Massey. James Reginald Massey has been identified by his Texas Driver's License # xxxxxxxx.

Most of the details regarding the investigation were not revealed to us. We were made aware of some things, in particular that Massey had changed his story. The obvious fact that he had cried out, "Someone shot my wife!" from the beginning made all of the legal team suspicious. His disrespect for the law made everyone's job difficult. He denied access to the house, and tried to control the whole situation. I find it hard to imagine such an out-of-control person attempting to manipulate a group investigation.

Supplemental Report: Officer R. Reynolds

On 04/09/95, at approximately 10:30 this Investigator, R. Reynolds 089, was contacted by Duncanville Police Communications in regards to a murder offense at 215 Hillcroft Dr. Duncanville, Dallas County, Texas. Communications officer B. Hyde, stated that he was calling for Sgt. J. Cowsert and that Sgt. Cowsert had requested my presence at 215 Hillcroft Dr.

This Investigator responded to 215 Hillcroft Dr. and made contact with Sgt. Cowsert. Sgt Cowsert requested that I obtain a Search Warrant for the residence, vehicles and person, James Reginald Massey. This Search Warrant also included trace and transfer evidence. Investigator Reynolds 089, prepared a Search Warrant and presented the same to Dallas County, District Judge Larry W. Baraka. Judge Baraka signed the Search Warrant at 2:15 a.m. on 04/10/95.

Investigator Reynolds 089 then returned to 215 Hillcroft Dr. and handed the Search Warrant to Sgt. Cowsert at the scene. Investigator Reynolds 089 remained at the scene for approximately 30 minutes and was released by Sgt. Cowsert. This Investigator never entered the residence and did not travel beyond the front sidewalk area.

From the beginning, our family had been reassured that everything within the scope of the law would be done. Equally, their focus was to bring this person to justice. The great lengths these investigators went to when writing reports verifies that fact. They were nearly listing and retracing every footstep. I am sure they had been in court and knew at some point all of the facts would be scrutinized by an attorney or group of attorneys. Each reporting officer really did take ample precautions when writing.

I actually have very fond memories of the officers involved. The circumstances were almost unbearable, but I knew I had to contain emotions to stay clearly on-message for my family. Ainley was the Detective who had phoned us early on Monday morning. Sgt. Cowsert was the lead investigator and reminded us of the actor Tom Selleck. He was very intense, and the idea that someone had committed such a brutal crime on a woman, especially one that he knew, really amplified his goal to put him away for a very long time.

Supplemental Report: Sgt. J. Cowsert

On 4-9-95 at approx. 9:49 p.m. I returned a page to the police department that was received on my pager. I was informed by Dispatcher Rene Kapraun that a possible shooting occurred at 215 Hillcroft and I was needed at the scene. At approx. 10:07 p.m. I checked in route and arrived at 10:20 p.m. I immediately was contacted at the scene by Lt. Spradlin and was advised that the victim was Pat Massey an employee at city hall. After being briefed of incident I contacted Lynda Staron of the DPD evidence room and advised her to contact Max Courtney of Forensic Consultants in Ft. Worth to process the crime scene.

I then met with Officer Beene who advised that a weapon had not been recovered. I then talked to Investigator Ainley who was assigned to the hospital where the victim was transported; this was at approx. 10:20 p.m. At that time Inv. Ainley advised that an entry wound could not be determined and that her skull was definitely cracked.

At approx. 10:20 p.m. I notified dispatch to contact Inv. Reynolds to come to the scene to assist with the investigation.

At approx. 10:25 p.m. I walked the perimeter of the residence and stood up on a wooden 6' fence that surrounded the back yard and part of the side of the house on the east. Over the fence in the back yard were an in-ground swimming pool and a swimming pool filter directly below the fence that I was looking over from.

At approx. 10:40 p.m. I recontacted Inv. Ainley who advised

that the victim was shot through the right cheek next to her nose.

Inv. Ainley advised that the victim's husband was at the hospital. I told Inv. Ainley that I requested DSO PIS and that they come to the hospital to conduct a hand wiping of Mr. J. R. Massey's hands.

Inv. Ainley advised that he asked Mr. Massey for consent to search the house and he advised "No, because he knows how you cops are."

I then contacted Inv. Reynolds who had arrived at the scene and advised him to go to the station and start working on a Search Warrant for the residence and hand wiping on Mr. Massey.

At approx. 10:55 p.m. I recontacted Inv. Ainley and he advised that J. R. Massey was demanding to be taken home. I instructed Ainley to have him escorted home.

At approx. 11:15 p.m. 4-9-95 Inv. McDaniel and Officer Moon arrived on the scene with J. R. Massey. Myself and Sims immediately approached J. R. Massey and asked if he would consent to a search of the house. He refused and said maybe he watches too much TV. He also wanted to know if what we were doing was legal, meaning having an officer posted at his front door and not allowing entry to the house. It was explained to him that we were in process of obtaining a search warrant and we are rightfully there. J.R. Massey refused a hand wiping by DSO and for us to collect his clothing until he consulted with an attorney.

He was provided a phone and his attorney's number and questioning stopped. All questions later concerning the investigation were directed through his attorney Lawrence Boyd who later showed up to the crime scene.

I then directed Inv. Sims to assist DSO and Forensic Consultants on obtaining subjs clothes and hand wiping after search warrant is obtained. I directed Inv. McDaniel to assist Forensic Consultants on the crime scene after warrant obtained.

I am recording the officer's statements as they were written. Paperwork can slow things down, and I know they were anxious to get this one completed. The forensic consultant team was only used in special cases. We were relieved to know they were being used. Keep in mind, this was during the Simpson trial and there was a lot of negative press on how that investigation had been botched. I can still feel the tension within the Duncanville Police Department. No one wanted anything to fall between the cracks. I am sure that after the way Massey acted, every officer involved wanted to personally slam the cell door behind him. From the way the officers recorded his statements and actions, I can feel their frustrations with having to deal with James Massey.

Supplemental Report: Officer Lynda Staron

On 04-09-95 at approx. 10:20pm R/O received a page from Sgt. Cowsert. Sgt. Cowsert informed me that a homicide had occurred at 215 Hillcroft Drive in our city. Sgt. Cowsert asked me to call out Max Courtney and his crime scene team from Forensic Consultant Services, in Fort Worth 817-870-1710 to the location to process the scene. R/O was told by Sgt. Cowsert that the victim was Patricia Pulley Massey, a secretary that was employed by the City of Duncanville and worked in City Hall.

Sgt. Cowsert instructed me to go to the station after I contacted Forensic Consultant Services, Inc. Until he coordinated everyone, and then he would tell me what else was needed.

I contacted Max Courtney at approx. 10:45pm from my residence and advised him that he was requested at 215 Hillcroft Dr. Max Courtney gave an ETA of about one hour and was given Sgt. Cowsert's mobile phone number to contact him for instructions.

At approx 11:10pm I arrived at the station. I was to type a search warrant for Inv. Reynolds of the residence where the victim's body was found, to include vehicles in the garage and also the person of James Reginald Massey (the victim's husband) which were all at 215 Hillcroft Dr. in Duncanville.

Inv. Reynolds called district Judge Larry Baraka at his residence who then signed the search warrant. Inv. Reynolds informed Sgt. Cowsert at the scene that the warrant had been signed, and that he was in route to the scene.

R/O left the station at approx 2:20am and went to 215 Hillcroft Dr. to contact Sgt. Cowsert. R/O arrived at the location and was contacted by Inv. Sims and Inv. Crawford who were already at the residence. R/O was told by Inv. Sims and Crawford that they were going to take the clothes the victim's husband was wearing into evidence, but that the majority of the evidence was going to Forensic Consultant Services, Inc.

Since I was no longer needed at the location to collect or store evidence I left the scene at approx 3:25am.

What an incredible view of an investigation in high gear. No one complains about the hours or the sense of urgency. The emphasis was placed on the importance of accuracy. I did not have the pleasure of meeting all of the officers involved, but something tells me that they all knew Mom one way or another and were working at 150 percent on her behalf.

"No stone left unturned" was the theme of this investigation. Officer Beene #081 was a patrol car officer who had been dispatched to the scene. Hindsight is always 20/20, so as you read this officer's report, bear in mind that no one knew exactly what had taken place. This is an actual account of a peace officer responding to a shooting call. Undoubtedly, his adrenaline was pumping at a rate most of us have never experienced. You can feel his pulse increase. His senses expand to hear, smell, and see absolutely every movement or shadow as he searches Mom's house. Mom's body is still face up on the floor of her bedroom. James Massey, her useless husband, has been outside running from house to house screaming, "She's been shot!"

Offense Incident Report: Patrolman Beene #081 Case #95002215. Description/Murder

4-9-95 R/O responded to 215 Hillcroft on a shooting. Upon arrival, R/O observed Ofc Moon and Mr. Massey in the front yard. R/O had received different radio reports that an armed male was at the scene.

R/O entered the residence and went to the NE master bedroom where Pat Massey was laying parallel to the sliding door, on her back, head facing south, face up with a wound to the front of her face and blood on the floor. Ofc. Holcomb advised that the rest of the house had not been checked.

R/O checked the west side of the house and found Pat Massey's purse dumped on the kitchen floor by the table and the sliding door to the back yard from the kitchen open. R/O checked the back yard and found nothing.

R/O then opened the washroom door and went to the interior garage door. When R/O opened that door, heat from the engines of the vehicle, (pickup and other vehicle) that were inside the closed garage, immediately hit R/O in the face. R/O checked the garage for susps/victims then notified Ofc. Holcomb that it was clear.

R/O had Ofc's Syptak & Livigni do a sweep of the exterior of the residence. R/O met Ofc. Moon and Mr. Massey in the front yard. R/O still had not accounted for the man w/a gun so R/O asked Mr. Massey if he was armed. He said "no" and R/O did a quick pat down of Mr. Massey to verify this.

R/O then went to 211 Hillcroft and met w/Jerry Sharb w/m [white male] stated that Mr. Massey came over beating on his front door. Mr. Sharb answered the door and Mr. Massey started yelling, "My wife's been shot call the police." Mr. Sharb grabbed his gun and met Mr. Massey outside the residence and would not let Mr. Massey go back into 215 Hillcroft. Mr. Sharb then went home and put up his gun–he had been the male with a gun.

#First observations of R/O: Master bedroom; body w/blood on floor, some type of table knocked over, purse dumped in kitchen, contents on floor. Kitchen door to back yard open with no apparent force, telephones appeared to be pulled out of walls. Both vehicles w/warm engines, garage door closed. #Mr. Massey had strong odor of alcohol about his breath and person and was upset.

R/O helped Ofc. Moon control Mr. Massey and get him into the front seat of Ofc. Moon's patrol car so he could be given a ride to the hospital behind the ambulance. R/O then parked in front of 215 Hillcroft to maintain front crime scene, R/O briefed CID upon arrival (Ofc. Holcomb was already in the house when R/O initially arrived. He stayed inside).

R/O knows Mr. Massey and his Ranger pickup from having issued him a speeding ticket previously. R/O knows Pat Massey from City Hall.

Investigator Ainley is the man who I phoned early on the morning of 4/10/1995. He is the person who had to tell us Mom had been shot and killed. I really liked Andy Ainley. He sort of put me in mind of a television detective named Andy. He wasn't too tall, had light hair, and always focused on the mission. He was so consumed with the case, I'm sure it kept him upset. His compassion for our situation was obvious, and, at times, it seemed to affect his behavior. His mission became ours: find everything we could to place James R. Massey away for a very long and difficult time in prison.

Supplemental Report: Detective A. Ainley

On 04-09-1995 at 10:05 pm this inv arrived at Charlton Methodist Hospital on a shooting call. This inv arrived just minutes prior to the ambulance with the deceased. The emergency room (ER) staff had already been notified that a possible gunshot wound was in route. The ambulance arrived. Immediately, the ER staff began to treat the deceased.

At 10:13 pm Dr. J Tsou, the attending physician, stated that he could not find an entry wound, but did note that the upper left back of the skull was fractured.

At 10:14pm Dr. Tsou stated that it appeared that spinal fluid was being pulled into the treatment tubes.

At 10:15pm the victim was pronounced dead.

At 10:17pm Dr. Tsou stated that the skull was definitely cracked and that there was still no point of entry to indicate a gunshot wound. Dr. Tsou decided that an X-ray was necessary.

At 10:37pm a possible gunshot wound entry point was discovered after the deceased had been cleaned. The wound was on the right cheek at the nostril. Dr. Tsou stated that the bullet must have impacted with the left upper area of the skull causing the fracture.

At 10:39pm the x-ray proved Dr. Tsou correct. The x-ray showed the bullet lodged close to the upper left area of the head. The X-ray also showed a straight line of fragmentation from the point of entry to where the bullet was lodged, traveling from right to left.

At 10:45pm this Inv. was present when Dr. Tsou advised Mr. Massey that the victim was deceased. This Inv. asked Mr. Massey what had happened. Mr. Massey stated that he had come into the residence through the garage, observed a light on in the bedroom, saw the deceased by the sliding glass door, and noted that she was covered with blood. Mr. Massey stated that he shook the deceased, placed his fingers on her throat to check for a pulse, ran to the residence next door and advised them to call "911."

When questioned about the whereabouts of the couple, Mr. Massey stated that he and the deceased had been to the Casa Blanca bar and restaurant at Red Bird Airport from 3:00pm until 5:00pm. Mr. Massey stated that they had gone to Cutters, a bar at 4107 Camp Wisdom Rd in Dallas. Mr. Massey stated that they each had a drink and went home. Mr. Massey could not remember any time frames after 5:00pm.

Mr. Massey was upset and this Inv. had Ofc. Moon get a box of tissues. Mr. Massey stated that she got very upset after they got home. Mr. Massey advised that when the deceased

THE SOUTHWESTERN INSTITUTE OF FORENSIC SCIENCES
AT DALLAS

Name_____ Autopsy No. *1103-95*

Color_____ Age_____ *Date_____

entrance

For protocol only:

2

95002215

COLT SINGLE ACTION REVOLVER .22 LR
MODEL - FRONTIER SCOUT
SER # - 11108K

FOUND PARTIALY BURIED
DIRT INSIDE BARREL
RED STAIN ON RIGHT SIDE GRIP

LOADING DIAGRAM

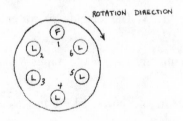

ROTATION DIRECTION

F = FIRED   1, 2, 3, 4, 5, 6 --- SUPER X
L = LIVE
E = EMPTY

HAMMER WAS DOWN
CYLINDER POSITION 1 WAS UNDER HAMMER

8-23-95
INV. G. M^cDANIEL

would get drunk, she would get upset over the loss of her first husband and become "feisty." Whenever the deceased was "feisty," Mr. Massey would leave the residence.

Mr. Massey did so on this date following the following route: Hwy 67 past Collins, back to Hwy 180. Stopped in a gas station on Hampton Rd. to buy a package of cigarettes, went to the Casa Blanca restaurant, found it closed, and went home to find his wife.

Mr. Massey advised that he has two guns in the residence. A ".38" and a .30-30 rifle. The deceased knew that the guns were kept in a closet in the bedroom.

At 11:10pm Mr. Massey was taken from the hospital to his residence by Inv. McDaniel and Ofc. Moon.

At 11:15pm this Inv. took photographs of the deceased.

At 11:25pm this Inv. collected the tissues that were used by Mr. Massey for any evidentiary purposes.

At 11:38pm this Inv. spoke with the field agent E. Rosenstrom of the Office of the Medical Examiners. This Inv. advised Mr. Rosenstrom of the current circumstances and advised him that this investigation required the most careful examination. Mr. Rosenstrom stated that this would be a trace investigation, indicating that any trace evidence would be sent to the proper places.

On 04-10-95 at 12:02am the deceased was released from the custody of this Inv. to David Duncan, who represented the Medical Examiner. Mr. Duncan and his associate transported the deceased.

At 12:20am this Inv. and Inv. Crawford went to Cutters, which is located at 4107 Camp Wisdom in Dallas, and spoke to Danny Pogue; w/m, and is a bar tender at Cutters. According to Mr. Pogue, the deceased and Mr. Massey were in the bar from approx.. 5:30pm until 6:30pm on 04-09-95. This is consistent with the only time frame given by Mr. Massey.
Mr. Pogue stated that Mr. Massey drank two scotches with a lemon twist and the deceased drank two vodkas with diet coke. Mr. Pogue advised that the two danced a dance. Mr. Pogue stated that the two persons appeared to be "getting along just fine." Mr. Pogue also stated that the two left alone.

On 04-09-95 at 4:12am this Inv. made contact with Jim Pulley, the son of the deceased. This Inv. stated, "I've got some bad news. Your mother has passed away." To which Mr. Pulley replied, "Did he kill her? ...... That son-of-a-bitch"… Garbled while speaking with his wife … "He killed her."

This Inv. was advised by Mr. Pulley that the deceased did not normally drink heavily, but would do so to make "him" feel better. The deceased would tell Mr. Pulley what she thought he wanted to hear. On 04-09-95 during the morning hours, the deceased had contacted Mr. Pulley to advise him that "everything was fine." Mr. Pulley stated that he would make the arrangements for his mother.

This Inv. again contacted E. Rosenstrom, the M.E., and was told that an autopsy would be performed at approx. 8:00am on 4-10-95.

This Inv. took the reel-to-reel tape of the initial call into evidence from the communications section on 04-10-95 at 5:00am and entered into evidence.

No further information at this time.

Most individuals have not gone through the emotions we were experiencing all at once. While writing Investigator Ainley's accounts of what occurred, it suddenly hit me that during all of this turmoil, Massey never once thought of or offered to call my brother or me. He was not the least bit concerned about anyone other than himself. Another fact brought out through Andy's statement was that Mom and I had spoken on Sunday morning. "Everything was fine." Maybe someone should write a song with that title.

When I say, "Detective Alvin Sims" aloud, I have flashes of very positive memories. He was a tall, dark-haired officer with a boyish look about him. Sims and I hit it off immediately. He wanted to find every possible bit of evidence on this thug. He had known Mom and really liked her, as a person and fellow employee. Sims had a good sense of humor. Oddly, an occasional laugh was something we all needed during that time. Now to add another layer of concern and fear, the neighbors had no clue as to what had actually taken place just a few doors down on their street. Poor Alvin was the one who had to answer to their concerns.

Supplemental Report: A. Sims

On the evening of 4-10-95, r/o and Inv. McDaniel met with three ladies in the front lobby of the station who were concerned with the homicide that had taken place in their neighborhood. We told them that we did not think there was a need to be alarmed about the situation and felt at that point that it was an isolated, associate type crime and not a crazy man just at random. One of the three stated that she had traveled west to east in the alleyway around 8:30pm-8:45pm and did not see anything unusual or any traffic in the alley. Another stated that she sat outside around 8:45pm maybe until 9:15pm and did not see or hear anything of concern, while she smoked a cigarette. The other female was one of the other's mother who did not have anything to offer. Both females stated that we might want to check with the people who live directly behind 215 Hillcroft. On 5-4-95 I called the resident who told me that they did not see or hear anything the evening of the murder. I asked her if she knew of any problems with the house behind her and she stated "no." I asked her if she knew either subject, and she stated that she knew Pat and "since she married I never had anything to do with her." I asked her if she knew him, referring to J. R. Massey and she stated "no." I asked her why she did not have anything else to do with Pat after her marriage to J. R. Massey and she stated that "I don't know." I asked her if it was just a gut feeling and she said "yes." I thanked her for her time and let her go. I believe that she might know a little more than what she told me.

Detective Sims spent a whole lot of time on the case. The total number of written reports from Sims is well over a dozen. Tracking everyone down, working in tandem with his fellow officers, he never once lowered his level of intensity.

Supplemental Report: A. Sims Date: 4/10/95 Time: 18:35

On 4-9-95, r/o was called at home and instructed to respond to a shooting call at 215 Hillcroft per Sgt. Cowsert at approximately 10:00 pm. R/o immediately began getting dressed and checked enroute to Duncanville at approximately 10:10 pm. While r/o was enroute to the location, I called and talked with dispatch about the situation at hand and was told that a woman had been shot and taken to the hospital and the husband had found her.

Bill Hyde told me that they had received the call from the neighbor, at 211 Hillcroft and they had not talked with the husband at all. Hyde also told me that the female had been pronounced dead. When r/o arrived at the location at about 10:30pm, r/o immediately met with Sgt. Cowsert outside the location. Ofc. Beene then met with myself, Cowsert and McDaniel in the street directly in front of the location.

Beene was informing us of the details that they encountered when they arrived at the location. Beene stated that Ofc. Holcomb and Ofc. Moon had gotten there at about the same and that they confronted Mr. Massey in between the houses, 215 and 211 Hillcroft, on his knees. Moon and Holcomb entered the residence and conducted a quick search for any suspects in the location and discovered the victim lying on the floor in the master bedroom, with an extreme amount of what appeared to be drying blood on the female's face and neck area. So much blood that they were not sure of what type of injury that the victim, who lied motionless and appeared to be without vital signs according to Holcomb.

When Ofc. Beene made it into the room, he called for investigators and realized that we had a big problem. According to Moon, he did not enter the room and he only stood at the threshold of the bedroom. Beene then ordered the crime scene secured and had been well handled by the looks of the location with police line tape wrapped around the front and back yard areas of 215 and at least the front yard area of 211 Hillcroft. Beene stated to me that Mr. James Massey, the husband to the deceased, had come home and found his wife "shot." Beene then relayed that "J. R." Massey went banging on the door at 211 Hillcroft and notified the listed witnesses, the neighbors, of what he had found.

I then went to the front yard area of 211 and made contact with them. After introducing myself to them, made our way into their residence at 211. This occurred at approximately 10:40pm inside 211 Hillcroft. I asked what they had seen and they both told me the story that at about 9:30pm, as they watched the Ten Commandments on TV, someone began banging very loudly on their front door to their residence and yelling. Jerry went to the door and opened it and observed a male he knew to be his next door neighbor at 215 Hillcroft, standing on his front porch and acting very odd and excited. Jerry invited J.R. into his house at which time J. R. continued to yell that, "Someone has shot my wife" and pleading for help.

His wife stayed inside her house and called 911 to report the shooting while Jerry retrieved his gun and went outside with J. R. who wanted to go back into the house at 215 Hillcroft. Jerry would not allow J. R. back into the house with fear of someone might still be inside the location.

Jerry and J. R. then started back to Jerry's house and J. R. stopped in between the two houses while Jerry continued into his own residence and put his gun back inside. R/o asked both neighbors to issue us with a written statement as to what had happened in this offense and their dealings with Mr. Massey. R/o asked them to write about anything unusual about Massey when he came into the location and Jerry's wife told me that "he just kept looking at his hands" while he continued to act upset and tell them that "his wife had been shot."

Jerry told me that while they were watching the TV, he was seated in his recliner chair, just inside of his back door which led out into the back yard. Jerry had his wooden door open and his storm glass door closed. According to Jerry, he stated that about 20-25 minutes before J. R. came knocking on his door, he observed a motion detector light come on in the alleyway that he thought might belong to his neighbor across the alleyway and a car's headlights head westbound in the alleyway. Neither stated that they had seen or heard anything odd in the area. Jerry told me that "if it was him leaving in the alley, he left in his Oldsmobile and not his pickup because it was a long car." After receiving the statements from the neighbors, r/o went back outside at 11:10pm and met back with Cowsert.

At 11:15pm, r/o observed a marked police unit pull up to the location with Ofc. Moon in the back seat, Mr. Massey in the car and r/o does not recall who was driving the squad.

When they exited, r/o initiated contact with Massey and told him that we were going to have to search his residence for any critical evidence and asked him for his consent on the search of the house and Massey then told me that "maybe I've watched too many TV shows but I think I might need to call my lawyer before I let you do that." I told Massey that we could not allow him to enter the residence because of it being a secured area and no one was allowed in at that time. I told Massey that we had an officer immediately inside the front door and the other perimeter officer was standing in the back driveway to the residence securing the back.

Massey also discussed that he would need to call his lawyer but he did not have his phone number and that it was inside the residence. R/o had Massey describe the location in which his "card file" was located and what it looked like. Massey told me that it was at the bar area in the kitchen in blue or black card holder. R/o went to the front door, remained outside the location and asked Ofc. Holcomb to go to the bar area and retrieve the card file. Ofc. Holcomb then brought back a blue card holder that was one of our police department card holders that contained his attorney's card.

I then offered to take Mr. Massey to my car and use my mobile phone to make any calls that he needed to make. We, Massey and I, went to my car and were seated in the front seat. I dialed the number for Massey since he did not have his glasses on or with him and after dialing the number, handed Massey the receiver. Massey then began talking with someone on the other end and eventually asked if I could step from the car so that he could talk with his attorney and I did.

When Massey got out of my car, he told me that his attorney was enroute to the location and he did not want to do anything until his attorney got there. R/o noticed on the card that his attorney was Lawrence G. Boyd with an office number of 691-5630.

At approximately 11:30pm, Det. Rowe with the Dallas Sheriff's office physical evidence section arrived at the location.

At 11:36pm, Cowsert made contact with Kent Trailor on the phone and asked if he could come to the location.

At approximately 11:50pm, Boyd showed up to the location and I introduced myself to him and told him that we had awaited his arrival so that we could obtain a consent to search on the house, obtain the clothes that Massey was wearing and ask for a hand washing from Massey.

Boyd told me that he would like to talk with" Jim" and walked off to his car. Boyd entered his driver's side and Massey entered the passenger's side of Boyd's car. After about 20 minutes they both got out of the car and r/o reapproached them both. Boyd told me that they did not have a problem with the consent to search on the house, any cars at the location and any adjacent buildings at the location but they did have a problem with me taking the clothes from Massey and the hand washings and would not allow it. I then told them both that we had an investigator at the station who was working on the search warrant and that if need be, we would wait on the search warrant to be signed. Boyd stated that we would wait for the warrant.

We, most officers on the scene and that were in the street talking, noticed several spots on the red shirt that Massey was wearing that appeared to be blood spots. R/o had heard from Holcomb that upon his arrival, Massey had told him that he went into the bedroom looking for his wife and when he found her lying on the floor, went over to her and reached down and felt for a pulse. After not feeling one, he ran from the location to the neighbor's house and got help. R/o did not feel that feeling of the pulse would have required getting several spots on his shirt that appeared to be spattered on the right, front side of his shirt. Two of the several spots that were located just above Massey's waistband were the larger two and appeared to have run downward for about ½ inch.

Massey argued with us in reference to "how long we were going to be in his house and whether or not he was going to need a motel for the night." Massey also expressed his concern and desire to use the restroom over and over, just before the arrival of Boyd. We told Massey that we would be in the house for at least 5-6 hours and we could not release one of his vehicles since they were parked inside the crime scene and in the garage. We did get with two neighbors and ask if they would allow Massey to use their restroom and they agreed, one being 219 Hillcroft.

When Boyd arrived, Boyd asked if he could take Massey for a ride and I told him that he could not leave with the clothes that he had on and we wanted them. Boyd did agree to allow Massey to use the restroom in the presence of the officers since he would not give up the clothes without the warrant. Ofc. Moon and Det. Rowe went with Massey to 219 Hillcroft and was gone very briefly. When they returned, Rowe stated that Massey only urinated for a very short time and did not appear to have to go very bad.

We continued to wait while Inv. Reynolds continued to work on the affidavit for the search warrant at the station. During this time, Boyd asked me what the crime scene was showing and I told him that we had not began the crime scene because we were waiting for the search warrant and that the only searching we had done had been for suspects and that was only an initial, quick search to allow the paramedics to enter the location in a safe manner, which maybe only lasted about 45 seconds to 1 minute. Massey then stated that "well I've been gone for about three hours and they've had officers in my house since I've been gone." I then turned my stream light flashlight on and lit up myself, Cowsert, Det. Rowe, Inv. McDaniel, Inv. Ainley and the three people from Max Courtney's group on the street and told Boyd that if a search was going on, we would be inside doing it instead of standing in the street twiddling our fingers.

I am not sure what time Reynolds notified us on the scene that he had completed the search warrant and had it signed by Larry Baraka and enroute to the location with it. Once

Reynolds reached the location with the warrant, r/o put on a pair of plastic booties at the door, along with a pair of gloves and a hair net and entered the location only to retrieve a pair of underwear, socks, pair of jeans, a shirt and another pair of boots for Massey since we were going to take the clothes that he was wearing.

I entered the residence and went to the master bedroom, to the chest of drawers that Massey had explained to me as being his, just inside the bedroom door on the immediate left. Massey told me to open the second drawer from the top for his underwear. I did so and found his underwear and removed one pair. Massey then told me that I could find his socks in the fourth drawer. I found them and only removed one pair as well. I noticed the bloody area around the sliding glass door in the bedroom and did not have to go within about 6-7 feet of the bloody area to reach his closet, which was inside his bathroom. The lights in the bathroom were not on so I used my flashlight and did not touch anything but the door knob on his closet.

While going through the master bedroom, the room looked as if there had been a physical confrontation in it. I observed two pictures hanging on the north wall hanging very crooked, a potted plant of some sort had been knocked over on the dresser on the right as you entered the room, a three or four tiered brass and glass round table knocked over that I had to step over to get into the bathroom doorway.

As I opened the closet door on the left in the bathroom, I observed men's clothing hanging inside. I reached up and removed one shirt that was hanging. I then removed one pair of black jeans, similar to the ones that Massey was wearing that evening and held them with the shirt. I then found a pair of boots and placed his underwear and socks in one of the boots. Just before leaving the closet, I looked up and observed about three or four boxes of ammunition boxes on the extreme left of the shelf in the closet.

Massey had told me earlier in the evening that he had two guns inside the location a 30-30 and a .38. I observed a box of .38 rounds and on top, a box of .22 caliber rounds of ammunition. The .22 ammunition box was turned slightly further to the right than the others on the end and the end of the box facing the door of the closet was opened. R/o became very concerned at that point because r/o had learned before that point that the gunshot appeared to be from a .22 caliber weapon and Massey had not stated anything about having a .22. R/o did not touch anything else and immediately left the residence.

I returned back to the front of the house and handed the clothes that I had gathered to Massey. I then called McDaniel and Cowsert over and told them about the box of .22 caliber ammunition on the shelf in his closet. I then met back with Boyd and Massey. Boyd asked me if Massey were to go with us to the station to obtain his clothes, would he be free to leave once we had done that and I told him yes that "this was no way any type of arrest and Massey would be free to leave." Boyd then asked me if I could bring him back home and I told him that I would. Boyd then told Massey that he would not come to the station but it would be okay to go with us.

I checked enroute to the station at 2:45am with "Tom" from forensics. Det. Rowe drove himself to the station with us. We went into the station and Tom took pictures of Massey while Rowe arranged his equipment to run a presumptive test on the spots on the red shirt worn by Massey and the hand washings. After Tom obtained his pictures needed of Massey in the clothes that he had been wearing and of his arms and hands, Rowe ran the swabs on Massey's hands.

We then had Massey remove his clothes over some sacks and we started with his shirt. I handed Rowe Massey's shirt and Rowe initiated a test on one of the larger spots which came back very quickly positive and very strong for blood. While the shirt lied on the table, r/o could see more spots on the shirt that had been noticed before. R/o observed several spots that were similar spotting as that had just tested positive and strong for blood. The closer the spots were to the top of the right upper chest area, the smaller the spots. As the spots got closer to the waistband area of Massey, the larger they became. There were even one or two spots on the back right portion of the shirt that could have been the same.

No other spots were tested and will be done so at the lab. Tom bagged the rest of the clothes as Massey dressed. Every single individual item removed were placed in their own individual brown paper sack and not touched together so that they would not contaminate each other.

After Rowe fingerprinted Massey for elimination purposes, we returned to the home address of Massey at 3:23 am on 4-10-95, about 40 minutes total time that he had been with us. After retuning to the location, Massey was still only concerned with when we were going to leave his residence and if he would have to get a motel for the night. I tried to get Massey to call a friend or work associate so that he could go with them and try to rest. Massey then stated that maybe he could stay with his neighbor, who had been very generous throughout the night with helping the officers and Massey with bathrooms and coffee and phone calls. Massey headed over to their house and wound up going inside.

Courtney's group and McDaniel were still processing the crime scene so I returned to the station and met with Lt. Spradlin, Cowsert, Beene, Holcomb and Ofc. Moon. I left the station at 6:00am for a short while. I had found out that the Medical Examiners office was going to perform the autopsy on Pat Massey between 8:00 and 8:30am on 4-10-95. I headed for the M.E.'s office at 7:30am.

I arrived at the location and met with the doctor who was going to perform the autopsy, Dr. Guileyardo and filled him in on what little bit of information we had about the crime scene. Guileyardo told me that dependant lividity normally begins setting up somewhere between 30 minutes and 2 hours depending on the temperature. I do not know if there had been very much lividity when the body was found but I had talked with Beene who stated that the blood on the victim's face was drying and the victim was no longer bleeding actively. Beene also stated that the blood that had pooled under the victim's head had congealed somewhat and turned a deep red almost purple color, indication that the blood had been somewhere around 15-30 minutes out.

At 8:55am, Guileyardo began the autopsy and estimated the muzzle range to be about 1 foot away from the right cheek area of the entry wound due to the "faint stipiling" around the entry wound. Technically, the Dr. stated that it could indicate that the muzzle of the weapon was somewhere from 1-3 feet away but he felt around 1 foot. He reported powder residue around the wound 1½ inches with no soot just powder particles.

At 9:24am, Dr. Guileyardo recovered a plain lead .22 caliber bullet from the back left upper portion of the victim's head, just under the scalp and outside of the skull. I observed the path of the bullet to be from the right cheek area headed upward and back traveling through the middle of the brain and exiting out of the skull before stopping.

The bullet was damaged on one side and very intact and non-mutilated on the other side long ways. Guileyardo even commented about the good chance of a successful comparison if the gun was found with the remarkable shape of half the bullet. Guileyardo also stated that a range could be determined really close if the gun used was found in determining estimated range of the muzzle from the entry wound. Guileyardo stated that there were no other apparent injuries on the victim that would indicate a very physical struggle before being shot. He also stated that a rape kit had already been performed on the victim and all of the trace evidence tests that coincide with it.

I asked Guileyardo about the possible blood spatters on the shirt of Massey and he told me that it could be from the victim coughing because of the profuse bleeding from such a head wound to her falling in his direction and the blood spilling out onto his shirt. He also stated that he would not say it couldn't happen on "blow back" but did not believe that it would be to the degree that I had relayed on the amount on Massey's shirt. Guileyardo also stated that he would not be surprised if the victim's hands came back positive for powder residue because of the chance of her being in a defensive mode with her hands up, not indicating that she fired the weapon, which had also already been performed.

Guileyardo further related that the make up of the lead bullet recovered seemed to possibly be significant because of it being all lead and not brass colored or "gilded" as most that they are seeing nowadays. Guileyardo stated that it "would be interesting to see what he has in his closet" on a comparison as to that bullet that was recovered from the victim's head. I left the autopsy after completion at approximately 9:50am.

I have stated that the Duncanville Police Department was very concerned over being detailed in their investigation. Some of the officers' reports cover the same timeframe. Reading each manuscript clearly shows everyone's unique perception of the crime scene. There are clues that were discovered which will come into play later.

Supplemental Report: Investigator G. McDaniel.
Report dated 04/09/95

This Inv. was paged and asked to respond to a shooting call at 215 Hillcroft. This inv. Responded to the Police Department and picked up a camera and crime scene kit. This inv. then arrived at 215 Hillcroft at 10:27pm.

This inv. observed that the crime scene had been secured and was taped off in the front and back by the crime scene tape. This inv. observed Ofc. Holcomb at the front door keeping the inside residence secure. This inv. met with Sgt. Cowsert and inv. Sims who were already on the scene. Sgt. Cowsert requested that this inv. meet with Inv. Ainley at Charlton Methodist Hospital where the victim had been transported. This Inv. arrived at Charlton Methodist Hospital at 10:47pm. This inv. provided inv. Ainley with a camera and inv. Ainley advised that the victim had been pronounced dead and that there was a bullet wound on the right side of the victim's nose. Inv. Ainley advised that an X-ray had been done and there was a bullet lodged in the head which appeared to be a small caliber. This inv. advised inv. Ainley that we would like to get consent to search the residence from victims husband, Mr. Massey.

The victim's husband came out of the family room with Ofc. Moon, who had transported Mr. Massey to the hospital. Inv. Ainley asked Mr. Massey if we could have consent to search to do a crime scene search. Mr. Massey said, "Yea, I guess so." And then said, "I know how you cops are, no, I want to talk to my attorney first."

Mr. Massey then asked if he could go in and see his wife and Inv. Ainley told him that he could not see her right now. Mr. Massey said that he either wanted to see her or he was going to leave. Inv. Ainley told Mr. Massey that it was not possible for him to see her right now and he would prefer Mr. Massey not to leave. Mr. Massey asked if he was under arrest and Inv. Ainley told him absolutely not. Mr. Massey said that he wanted to go home and asked how he was going to get there. This Inv. and Ofc. Moon gave Mr. Massey a ride back to 215 Hillcroft.

Mr. Massey said very little on the ride back. Mr. Massey said that he had some calls he needed to make and would sob from time to time. This inv., Ofc. Moon and Mr. Massey arrived back at 215 Hillcroft at approximately 11:15pm.

This Inv. was advised that Inv. Reynolds was at the police station preparing a search warrant.

Mr. Massey asked to use this Inv. mobile phone and sat in this Inv. car and made some phone calls. This Inv. gave Inv. Sims a copy of consent to search the residence that this Inv. had started filling out at the hospital. Inv. Sims got with Mr. Massey and his attorney Larry Boyd, who had arrived at the scene after apparently being contacted by Mr. Massey.

The Consent to Search was completed and signed by Mr. Massey and his attorney at 1:05am on 4-10-95. At this time the search warrant was close to being completed and it included hand washings and clothes from Mr. Massey and it was decided by Sgt. Cowsert to wait for the warrant to be signed.

At 2:25am, inv. Reynolds arrived at 215 Hillcroft with the signed search warrant. This Inv. was assigned by Sgt Cowsert to assist and observe the crime scene search conducted by Forensic Consultant Services. The people involved in the search with this service were: Max Courtney, Tom Ekis and Jon Brooks. This Inv. along with Max Courtney did a preliminary walk-through inside the residence after with protective footwear.

This Inv. noticed there were no apparent signs of struggle in the living room and there was food on a paper plate on the coffee table. In the master bedroom there were two significant pools of blood near a sliding glass door and dresser. There were packaging from the medical supplies on the floor that paramedics had apparently used when working on the victim. In the breakfast area adjacent to the kitchen there was a purse with its contents scattered on the floor beneath the table area. Max Courtney pointed out some shiny areas on the area around the sliding glass door lock. This door was partially open and led to the patio. This Inv. remarked to Mr. Courtney that these marks appeared to maybe be internal markings. Mr. Courtney advised that these marks would be examined later when the door could be closed to determine if they were internal or a sign of forced entry. The back yard and pool area appeared undisturbed with the exception of a small piece of wood that was on the fence which was a 6' Stockade fence.

At approximately 3:35am Mr. Courtney began recording a compact video cassette tape of the scene while Mr. Ekis took color photographs of the scene. A detailed search was then performed by Courtney, Ekis, and Brooks assisted while this inv. observed.

In the master bedroom, two blood pools that appeared to be still wet were on the carpet near the sliding doors. The larger of the stains was closer to the sliding doors. There was a small amount of blood at the bottom of the door curtains. A piece of clothing material, apparently cut from a shirt, was found on the floor near the blood pools. A metal plant stand with glass shelves was found on its side close to the bathroom door. One of the glass shelves was broken.

An alarm clock was found on the floor beneath a small table. The clock was unplugged and the time shown was 7:59. The clock was checked by Ekis and when it was plugged in, it appeared to work. A white, woman's shoe was found on the floor near this table. Next to the table was a cloth chair, behind this chair there was a telephone jack that contained a plug that the wires had been apparently pulled from.

On the south wall, a small pot with decorative branches was lying on its side and it appeared to have recently been knocked over. In the bathroom area of the master bedroom, there was a closet on the west end that contained men's clothes. On the floor of the closet there was a .30-30 rifle and a .16 gauge shotgun.

On the top shelf, on the south side of this closet, were boxes of ammunition. This included a partial open box of .22 long rifle cartridges, a box of .25 auto cartridges, and a box of .30-30 cartridges. There was another box that contained two (2) plastic bags of .38 special cartridges. Also found on the shelf was a gun cleaning kit and a box containing a .38 cal. Rossi revolver loaded with four (4) cartridges, three (3) .22 cartridges were found on the floor beneath the box of .22 cartridges that were on the shelf.

A cowboy boot was found on the right side of the back shelf that contained an orange towel. Inside the towel were a Raven .25 auto pistol inside a plastic bag and a magazine with six (6) .25 cartridges. On the outside of the closet door there was a caved-in portion which appeared to this inv. to have possibly been made by striking the door with a fist.

On the opposite end of the bathroom was a closet containing women's clothing. In the hallway of the residence, this inv. observed a piece of tissue paper on the floor and a vacuum cleaner standing in the hallway.

In the middle bedroom there was a sofa and TV set. On the sofa, was a pillow and sheet. In the front bedroom there was a bed and a bed table containing personal papers, a telephone with a broken cord was on the floor near the door to the bedroom. A small piece of the telephone cord was found plugged into a jack on the baseboard of the bedroom closet just inside the door. One end of this cord also appeared to be broken.

In the hall bathroom, on the vanity, was some tissue paper containing pinkish-colored lip imprints. The door to the bathroom had been forced open and there was a crack in the frame near where a striker plate had been. The striker plate was lying on the vanity next to the bathroom door.

In the living room, on the coffee table, was a paper plate containing what appeared to be potato chips and possibly the remains of a sandwich or similar food item. Also, on the coffee table was a tape titled, "Wild Orchid II." The video tape appeared to be completely re-wound.

On a stuffed chair on the north wall there was a plastic video tape box sitting on an Albertson's sack. Inside this sack was a tape invoice from Albertson's #4268, 4104 Wheatland Rd., invoice #1-0026. The invoice appeared to have a signature by Mr. Massey and was dated 04-09-95.

At 7:28pm in the kitchen area, on the counter next to the refrigerator was an uncut block of yellow cheese and a paper plate containing crackers, along with a small kitchen knife. On the breakfast bar there was a telephone that first appeared not to work. The redial function was pushed and dialed 1-800-347-2683 and it was determined that this was a customer service line for Discover Card.

A credit card billing from Discover with the telephone number was found on the breakfast bar. In the breakfast area a purse lay on the floor at the bottom east side of the breakfast table. The contents which included a billfold were scattered on the floor around the purse.

The table contained a briefcase and numerous papers. The sliding door was closed and examined and it was determined that there were no apparent pry marks.

Inside the garage were two vehicles, a 1994 maroon Ford Ranger truck, bearing Texas license plate KA9651. On the east side of the garage was a maroon Olds Delta 88 bearing Texas license plate GGR11N. All windows were found to be secured, the patio door in the master bedroom was locked and the overhead garage door was secure.

The house was darkened and Ekis processed the floors of the bedroom and hallway with Luminol reagent. Mr. Courtney advised that the luminescent patterns that were indicated on the floor of the master bedroom were suggestive of body outlines around the area of the blood pools. Luminol reagent was also processed inside the Ranger pickup truck. A hand towel on the console was noticed to contain luminescence when sprayed lightly by Ekis.

Attached to this report is a list of evidence collected by Courtney, Ekis, and Brooks.

Ofc. Broussard and Ofc. Brannen arrived at approximately 8:50am on 4-10-95 and searched the attic portion of the house due to disturbed dust found at the base of the attic stairway in the hall when it was pulled down. Nothing of significance was found in the attic.

At approximately 8:06am on 04-10-95 Ofc. Ivy #106 checked the alleyway area behind 215 Hillcroft. Nothing of significance was found in the alleyway.

At approximately 11:34am on 4-10-95 this inv. was relieved at the crime scene by Inv. Ainley. Investigation continues.

Having read through all reports, I still say they left no stone unturned. All of these police reports are a fine example of a well-oiled investigative machine. We had no idea what was taking place inside Mom's home as we traveled from our house. The detectives thoroughly filled us in once we had arrived at the police station on the morning of April 10, 1995.

Reading over these reports brings back vivid memories of how my mother lived. The officer's description of the inside of her house tells me quite a bit. My mom was meticulous with how she kept her personal records. The reporting officer/detective noted the Discover bill out on the table. I can only assume that an argument started over some unexpected charges James Massey had placed on the credit card. Mom apparently called the service center to confirm those items purchased. April 9, 1995, was a Sunday. Mom always made sure she was home early to be prepared for work the next day. The clock in the master bedroom showed 7:59 p.m. The mental picture I get is of that clock flipping as it changed time. The model was the type that had the little plates; no LED in the '70s, and that clock had been around a year or two. Mom liked to snack at night. The cheese left on the counter was undoubtedly hers. I can say in all certainty that only one gun was in that house the day my father died. The .16-gauge shotgun had not been fired since New Year's Day of 1973. Dad traditionally stepped out the back door at midnight to fire a round in the air. Once the smoke cleared he would shout, "Happy new year!" The pistols and the 30-30 rifle must have scared the daylights out of Mom. She always despised any type of firearm.

The detective also described how Mom's purse had been dumped on the floor. This turned out to be a weak attempt at an alibi from Massey. "Someone came into the house while I was returning a movie." This was only one of several varying statements from James R. Massey on the night of April 9.

I would like to share one more report with you. It is a continuation of an earlier report from Detective Sims. The dates and times take us into the depths an investigator will go to get all the details of a crime. Reporting is essential to building a sound case against an accused person. Mom was a friend of Sims; he and I had spoken about it during the week of the funeral. Reading his report reminds me of the determination he spelled out to us all. No one ever complained about the hours, phone calls, or legwork required to put James Massey where he belonged.

Supplemental Report: Time: 21:28 Reporting Officer: Sims A.

I failed to mention all that was involved in the consent to search request of 215 Hillcroft on the night of the offense, 4-9-95 and the dealing with Mr. James Massey and his attorney, Lawrence Boyd.

We had submitted them with the consent to search form and Boyd took possession of it and requested time to speak with his client, "J. R." Massey, in private. Both Boyd and J. Massey went to Boyd's car and were seated in the car. After about 20 minutes, they both got out of the car and Massey had signed the bottom of the consent form. R/o requested that each individual blank of the form be initialed by Massey along with putting the date and time on the sheet that had not been filled out.

They again had re-entered Boyd's car to talk and I asked them to do those things as they talked. The next time they stepped out, the form had been completed with consent to search the house. We then discussed the possibility of us taking possession of James Massey's clothes and hand wiping and was asked by Boyd why we would want that. I told Boyd that we would request it from anyone for obvious reasons. J. Massey had been inside the residence and we wanted to try to preserve any and all possible trace evidence from the crime scene and that he had entered that scene and left, possibly taking some evidence with him and or if nothing else, to eliminate J. Massey as a suspect.

Boyd then told me that they could not allow the clothing to be taken or the hand washings conducted. I then told Boyd that we would wait for our search warrant that was in the making that would include everything. Boyd then asked me if he could take J. Massey for a ride and talk with him. I told Boyd that J. Massey was not free to leave with the clothes on his back or without surrendering them to police and the hand washings conducted.

Boyd did not disagree with that and we waited until about 2:45am on 4-10-95 for the search warrant to get on the scene by Inv. Reynolds who had been the affiant on the warrant and would often call out to the crime scene and obtain information from officers as needed.

I also spoke with the other next door neighbor who lived at 219 Hillcroft at 2:20am, who told me that he had known Pat for some time while she lived at the residence by herself, before she met Jim, and that she was a very kind lady. He also stated that they did not hear anything at all and that he was not aware of any problems between the couple but then again, did not see them a whole lot.

On 4-10-95, I called and talked with Dr. Guileyardo about the chance of printing the victim's body for latents and he told me that he did not think that it would benefit because of the victim being in the refrigerator and it was not very favorable even if she had not been cooled down. Guileyardo directed me to call Roger Smith, the fingerprint expert for the M.E.'s office.

I talked with Smith who told me that if printing the body was ever considered, it would need to be done immediately upon finding the body and that at this point and time, it would not be possible. Smith also pointed out that if Jim Massey's prints were on the body, he was the husband and that would not be unusual.

R/o got back in touch with Boyd by phone and asked him if they were going to meet and come talk with me as he had stated earlier on wanting to know some details himself and that he thought it would be important that Massey relay some of the information before he forgets where he went and who was working. Boyd told me that once he talked with Massey, he would call me back but he would like to get a copy of the body of the search warrant affidavit and then talk with Massey.

Our records division had told him on the phone that they could not release it because the case was an open case. I told Boyd that I did not know one way or the other but I would find out and if it was possible to release the affidavit, that I would see to it that it was released. I later called back to Boyd and he told me that they, he and Massey, would come into my office on 4-11-95 at 2:00pm and sit down and talk with us. Boyd also told me that he would obtain the copy and then come back.

On 4-11-95 at 1:37pm, I received a call from Boyd who stated that Massey had called his office before he had gotten in and stated that he would call back and had not done so nor had Massey left a message as to what motel he was in or a return number. Boyd then stated that Massey was not aware of the 2:00pm appointment and, therefore, they would not be at the meeting.

I then became upset with Boyd and told him that I was not getting cooperation from Massey with regards to anything in trying to assist clearing him. I asked Boyd what the concern was with the search warrant and he told me that he wanted to determine who was suspect. I told him that everyone was suspect including the postman and that we were trying to eliminate Massey and he was not wanting to help us do that. I told Boyd that we had considered all possibilities including Massey's involvement and he was not cooperating with us at all and that maybe we needed to look harder his way because of the way he was acting that was causing me to raise an eyebrow. Boyd stated that he was concerned because of the past abuse problems. I told Boyd that just because of the past problems that did not make him guilty of the murder.

I further told Boyd that if anything happened to my wife, whether or not we had had a knock-down drag-out and I left and returned to find her in the manner that he found his wife, that I would assist the police in any way whatsoever. If it meant giving them my clothes, so be it. If it meant super gluing my house and being inside for days, so be it because I would want the son of a bitch caught that did that to my wife. Boyd stated that he understood where I was coming from and that "they had several options and once he talks with Jim after viewing the search warrant, they would decide on which option that they would take and get back with me." I told him my beeper number again and told him that it was on 24 hours a day, just let me know and I would work with them in any way.

I had also called the Freeway Pawn Shop on Ovilla Rd. in Red Oak and talked with the person working on 4-10-95 and had him check to see if Jim Massey had bought, sold or pawned anything and he told me that he could see a $255.22 purchase but he could not give me the date or what was purchased and that I would need to talk with the owner of the shop on 4-11-95.

On 4-11-95, I called the pawn shop back and talked with the owner who told me that the purchase was for a Rossi .38 caliber revolver that was purchased on 1-19-94 and that he had no other activity since that date on Jim Massey.

We, McDaniel, Ainley and myself, went to the Red Bird Airport to contact a possible witness that McDaniel had discovered about a possible .22 handgun that Jim Massey might have had. We went to the location and met the witness who told us verbally and in a written statement that sometime between Thanksgiving and Christmas of 1994, Jim Massey entered into a conversation about guns and stated that he, Jim Massey, had a 30-30 carbine and a handgun for sale and wanted to know if he was interested in buying either. The witness told him that he might be interested in both.
He believes that originally he understood the handgun to be

a .45 style, as Massey described it. The next conversation he noted the Winchester model 84 with a serial number of 1650598 and determined that it was manufactured in either 1949 or 1950. Once he asked Massey what he wanted for the gun, Massey decided that he did not know what to ask for the gun and he would just hang on to the gun.

During the subsequent conversations, Massey then described the handgun to this witness as being a .45 type western style "cowboy" revolver but was in fact a .22-caliber gun. He noted the serial number and issued it to us and did not purchase either. This was a key statement, written statement in that he could put Massey in possession or at least in a conversation where he claimed to have possession of a .22 handgun that might be the reason .22-caliber rounds were found in Massey's closet. While at the location, R/o went inside the bar/restaurant area and issued a card to the bartender who told me that some of her friends saw Pat and Jim in the location having arguments over the weekend. I issued her with my card and told her that if anybody knew anything about the Masseys, to please have them call me.

After Ainley and McDaniel received the statement from the witness, we left and returned to the station. I then called ATF and issued them with the serial number and had them run a check on the number. After about 30 minutes, they called me back and told me that their records did not go back to 1949 or 1950 and could not help me track the 30-30. We were trying to track the 30-30 to the original owner because the witness believed Massey bought the 30-30 and the .22 from the same guy in Duncanville at one of the social clubs that he frequented.

I then went to the Gold Rush which is a bar on Gannon in Dallas just outside of Duncanville and contacted a man there that told me that he had only bought the club about 1 week prior to me showing up from a man named Phil, who owns a club named O'Malley's on Zangs in Dallas. This man issued me with a work number. I called the work number and spoke to a bartender at O'Malley's who used to bartend at the Gold Rush. She told me that she knew why I was calling and that she did know Pat and Jim Massey well. I also asked her if the owner was in and she told me "yes." I told her that I would be there shortly to talk with both of them about the Masseys.

When I arrived at the location on 4-11-95 at about 4:50pm, the bartender told me that all that she knew was that Jim drank a lot and that she had only heard of possible abuse to Pat from Jim. She also told me that the owner had left the location to obtain items for a big fish fry that they were going to have during the evening at the club. I did not stay there long.

After returning to the office, I received a call from a bartender at the Red Bird Airport, Anke Van Pelt, w/f, who told me that she observed Pat and Jim Massey arguing over who was going to pay this month's bills. I returned back there and received a written statement from her along with copies of outstanding bar tabs that Pat and Jim Massey had ran up on Saturday 4-8-95 and Sunday 4-9-95, the day of the offense.

On 4-9-95, it shows that Jim Massey ordered and drank 7 scotch on the rocks and Pat had drank 4 vodka and diet coke and one plain coke. On 4-9-95, Florence Montoya worked the bar and she also called me when I returned to the office and met with Anke. Montoya told me that on Saturday evening, there were only about 4 people in the club, 2 men and Pat with Jim Massey. Just before they left, Florence Montoya observed Jim Massey grab Pat by the back, neck of her shirt and pull her backwards to him. Florence stated that she asked Pat if she was Okay and Jim answered her with "Yes, she's fine." Florence then observed both return to their seats after coming from the bathrooms and after about 5 seconds, Pat got up and left the bar. Florence tried to tell her goodnight and Pat had nothing to say to her, which was very odd because Pat was never like that to anybody. Jim continued to drink his drink. Florence asked Jim if she needed to go check on Pat and Jim told her, "No, she just has a bad headache." Florence stated she realized then that Pat was a mistreated woman because she saw the fear in Pat's eyes when Jim had her from behind and by the neck of her shirt in his clinched fist.

Florence then stated that on 4-9-95 Pat and Jim Massey came into the location about 2:30-3:00pm. Florence told me that he, Jim, had a lot more to drink than her and that he always drank scotch on the rocks and not diluted. When they got ready to leave, Jim asked her to just give him just ½ of a shot of scotch. Florence stated that he had helped her at one point so she gave him just ½ of a shot of scotch. After doing so, Pat stated for "Flo" to give her just ½ shot of vodka, so she did and they both left around 5-6pm.

Florence met with Sgt. Cowsert on the evening of 4-11-95 and issued him with a written statement of these facts.
I then continued on paperwork. I then decided to call Carroll Roofing, where Jim Massey stated that he worked. I spoke to

a man who I told that I needed to talk with the owner who, he told me, was Ronnie Carroll. I left my number to have him call me.

After about ten minutes, I received a call from Ronnie Carroll. I told Carroll that I understood that Jim Massey worked for him and he said, "No, not really." I then asked if it was only when he wanted to and he said, "yes" and that he had not talked with Massey in over a week until the last ten minutes, and that Jim Massey had called him.

I asked what was said and Carroll told me that Massey had told him that he would not be back in to work and that he had some contracts on roofs that if he would get in touch with me, that I would assist him in obtaining them back but not to call me until 4-12-95. Massey went on to say that it was an accident and that they were both drunk and when they got home they got into an argument and Pat told him to leave and he said, "no." He then told Carroll that Pat went and got his gun from under the bed and when he tried to take it away from her, the gun went off and struck her.

I told Carroll that I needed to talk with him as soon as possible. Carroll told me that he was willing to help and I told him that we would come to his house because we needed to get a statement from him. Carroll invited us on out to do it. McDaniel and I headed his way about 8:00pm on 4-11-95.

We went to Carroll's house in Mesquite and he began writing his statement which stated the above plus that Pat Massey used to call him and say that Jim would get drunk and chase her around the house with a gun and tell her that he would kill her if she ever tried to leave him. Pat had also told Carroll that she knew she had to leave him and that she had already opened a bank account without Jim on it and that was the first step in trying to get away.

Jim Massey also told Carroll that he could not tell Carroll where he was staying because the police were looking for him and that he would not even be able to go to Pat's funeral. At the end of the conversation, Massey stressed to Carroll not to call me until 4-12-95 because his mother was flying in from California and he wanted to see his parent. With this statement, McDaniel and I headed back to the station where we were to begin putting together an arrest warrant for murder for Massey.

Once we arrived at the station, Cowsert, Spradlin, Ainley and Reynolds were there and Reynolds had already begun to type the affidavit. McDaniel assisted in the affidavit. Cowsert called Discover Card and found out that $500.00 had been obtained off of his card in Desoto on 4-11-95 at 12:18pm.

Cowsert and Spradlin set out around 10:30pm to try to look at motel lots in Desoto for Massey's car. We also feared that he may be trying to flee, maybe to California, in the way that he was arranging things or his personal matters and maybe trying to buy time in not having Carroll to call me until 4-12-95.

We figured, since Massey liked to drink, that they should start at the Holiday Inn in Desoto because they had a bar. About ten minutes after they left, Cowsert called back to the office and said that they had found his car outside the Holiday Inn. Cowsert and Spradlin sat on the car until the warrant was completed and signed by our magistrate with a bond at $200,000. McDaniel, Ainley, and I then headed to their location to assist.

We arrived at about 3:15am at the Holiday Inn at Hwy 35 & Wintergreen Rd in Desoto. Lt. Spradlin called for a supervisor with the Desoto PD and a Lt. from their department responded and met with us. We discussed our options and concluded that we would try to wake him. We discovered, at the front desk, that he had asked for a 7:00am wake up call. We went back out and I sat with Spradlin and Cowsert while Ainley and McDaniel sat together in vehicles maintaining surveillance on Massey's vehicle.

We had also decided to have the Desoto Tactical Team respond to the location around 6:00am and wait for the movement of Massey to serve the warrant. I was assigned to the Desoto Tactical Van and sat with the team of 6 officers led by Lt. Broadnax. At approximately 7:20am, before I began thinking of Massey ordering room service the two mornings before for breakfast and told Broadnax that maybe if he was to order room service, we could serve his breakfast. I said this because when Massey was given his wakeup call, he asked what time check out was and we did not want to have to wait an additional 4 hours.

Broadnax called into the Hotel and spoke with an officer who had been posted behind the service desk and out of sight in the office area and told him that if Massey calls for room service to let us know. I then radioed Spradlin and Cowsert and asked them the same and Cowsert told me that it would be Desoto's decision to make. About 5 minutes later, Broadnax was notified on his radio to call back into the officer behind the desk, which he did. Broadnax received information on that call that Massey had just ordered room service for breakfast.

We, the tactical van occupants, began to move into the stairwell and meet with the plain clothes officer that was on the inside, where we met and discussed what would take place. The female who had been assisting us all night working the front desk would be the one to act as if she was delivering the breakfast and knock on the door with a tray, then step out of the way and the tactical team, who had been deployed on each side of the door into #334 would rush Massey when he opened the door. This plan was devised by Lt. Broadnax of their department.

At approximately 7:40am, the female knocked on the door and as the door began to open, the tactical team rushed Massey and took him into custody without incident. I then made entry into the room and radioed to Cowsert to have our guys come in. I discovered suicide notes that Massey had hand written lying around on the dresser and the television after I assisted Massey up and into a seated position on one of the beds from his face down position on the floor. Cowsert, Ainley, McDaniel and Ettessam made their way into the room.

Cowsert began to pick up all Massey's personal property and place it in a bag and then place the handwritten notes in another bag. We walked Massey down the stairway and I asked Massey if he knew why he was arrested and he said no.

I told him that he was under arrest for the murder of his wife.

Just before we exited the door, Massey began to complain of a sharp pain under his left eyebrow. I had an ambulance called to the location by Cpt. Johns of Desoto Police. The ambulance arrived and checked Massey's blood pressure, blood sugar, heart rate and rhythm and everything, according to the paramedics, was fine and they would not transport because of it being a minor problem and they did not think of it being of such nature to transport. After Massey sat through the examination, I asked him how he was feeling and he said much better and he never complained again.

I think that it might be possible that the bright light of the sun, on the cloudless day affected his eyes and was having trouble getting used to the light. After some time in it, he didn't say anything else. I rode with Ofc. Ettessam as he transported Massey to jail and assisted in the book in.

The only thing said the entire time about anything close to the situation was Massey told me that he had checked with Boyd on 4-11-95 and he said at that time there was no warrant out for him and wanted to know when we got the warrant. I told him that it was signed just before 3:00am and he said that "it sure didn't take you long to find me." I asked Massey if he wanted to talk about anything that had gone on and he said that he better talk with Larry first. I said that was fine. Nothing else was talked about during the transport or book in process in regards to this offense.

On 4-12-95, Jim Pulley asked us if we would check with Massey and see if he would be willing to release the dead bolt key to 215 Hillcroft. I went back in the jail and asked Massey if he would be willing to release the key to Jim Pulley and he said yes he would. Massey told me that he would have to see his key ring.

Eddie Edwards removed the key ring from his property and as I held them up, he told me which key it was. Once I removed the key from the ring, Massey asked me to go to the house and get him some more clothes and the property was in the third dresser drawer. Since Massey asked me to go to the house and get those items and Jim Pulley did not mind, myself and McDaniel went to the location and I boxed up the new underwear and socks that were on top of his dresser and everything out of the third drawer, as Massey requested. I also went to his closet and removed one shirt and one clean pair of jeans for him, as he requested.

While I was in the bathroom in the master suite, I observed the gun case that contained the 30-30 that was in question on a witness's written statement and began to wonder what the serial number was on the gun that Massey had there and if it was in fact the gun that he tried to sell to the witness. If it was the same, it would add credibility to this witness's statement which implicated J. R. in possession of a .22-caliber handgun.

I opened the case and removed the gun with Jim Pulley's permission to look at it and Pulley stated that his dad used to own one and he wondered if this gun was the one his dad owned. I removed the gun from the case and it was in fact the same model, make and serial number that the witness was shown and he considered buying, a Winchester model 84 with serial number of 1650598, and after Pulley looked at the gun, stated that it was not the gun that his dad used to have. We left the location with J. R.'s property and I had Eddie Edwards place the items in Massey's property.

Chapter Ten

Second Wind

FUNERALS ARE EXHAUSTING. EVERYONE NEEDED some space on Thursday the thirteenth, so we all rested at the hotel after Mom's service. The investigation was obviously running at full speed. As you can see from the officers' reports, I was very much involved. Friday was going to be another full day. All of my immediate family knew we were going to empty Mom's house, but none of us were aware of the behind-the-scenes proceedings.

On April 12, investigators received a call from a person Massey had called from his hotel room. This so-called friend of his had talked with him the night before. He was told, by Massey, that there had been a fight. Again, he tried to put it off on Mom telling his buddy she had gotten the gun from under the bed. She was waving the pistol in his face, and when he grabbed the gun she latched on to his shirt. According to Massey, once she did that, she pulled him over on top of her, and the .22 revolver fired a shot, which hit Mom in the right side of her face. Massey never told any of this to law enforcement. He contended that he had left, come back, and found Mom face-up on the master bedroom floor.

Investigator Reynolds was able to contact Massey's first wife on the fourteenth of April. She told him some things that were very shocking.

The two had been divorced for over ten years. Massey had never laid a hand on this woman. He had found some sort of pleasure in a $1,000-per-day cocaine habit. Her biggest fear was the type of people supplying him with his drugs. She turned him in to the DEA and filed for divorce. Massey left Florida right after the two separated. The family he abandoned never received a dime in child support. This information explained why his eldest daughter never had anything to do with him again. Jamie, the youngest, held on to a weak relationship, presumably due to her grandmother's involvement. His mother was the one propping up Massey financially. This woman even offered three pieces of property as collateral to bond her little baby boy out of jail.

Later in the day on Friday, April 14, Massey's family appeared in court. The original bond was set at $200,000. We were fine with that, though the amount still seemed low. During the legal procedure his family made it clear to the judge that they had $7,500 in available cash, not including the three pieces of land. Bailing a person out of jail requires 10 percent of the total bond. Only one negative thing was mentioned in court concerning Mom's family: Massey's daughter told Judge Hampton that I had threatened her dad. What would a reasonable person expect? The court, in all of its wisdom, promptly lowered his bond amount to $50,000. Little did we know that our legal system is motivated by the almighty dollar. The first day of proceedings proved to be lesson one for my entire family and me. James Massey was again free to roam the streets.

The evidence seemed to continue pouring in to the police. Mom's sister, Shirley, turned over four letters to the investigators. All four were signed and dated. Signing and dating was typical of Mom. Her background in record-keeping seemed to be motivating an attempt to document the abuse she endured. The dates on her letters ranged from a few weeks after he had beaten her in January of 1994 to three weeks before he shot and killed her in April of 1995. The letters either pointed to his alcohol abuse or her desire to leave him. She signed one of the letters *Patricia L. Pulley*. Choices made by others that don't have any rationale are deeply difficult to comprehend. Mom perpetually turned the other cheek, as if to say, "Come on, I know you will change."

As I walked into work that Monday morning on April 17, I felt like I had been in a car wreck. My energy had been sucked out of me by the battery of emotions I had been submitted to. Feelings of self-pity, depression, anger, even helplessness pulsated throughout my system with every step. One of my coworkers commented that he felt I should turn around and go home. The little man I answered to never even acknowledged that I had been through such an experience. Life goes on, and so did my J.O.B. All of my concentration had been overrun by the reality of a loved one's life being taken in such a violent manner. Mentally I relived every event of the past week. Each day flew by while I paid very little attention to detail. My slow but steady spiral into depression was methodically creeping into my soul. Nothing in life mattered. People generally find something to numb the pain; my relief came from a beer can. Many, many aluminum-encased pain relievers were consumed.

At home, I had put Mom's personal papers in a box, strategically placed by my recliner. Every night, I would scan through the documents looking for clues. I actually found a few. On the evening of April 17, I phoned the Duncanville police station to notify them that I had found out Massey had been using two Social Security numbers. Jack and I had made plans to follow up with the police on the twenty-fourth, so I promised them I would deliver these documents to them at that time. My evenings were spent making phone calls and organizing all of the paperwork. The makeshift filing cabinet at the side of my easy chair almost consumed me. Tuesday night, Mom's Merrill Lynch broker revealed to me that two large sums of money had been withdrawn over the past two years. This lady had the undesirable opportunity to meet, or confront, Massey. During both meetings, she said, he was drunk and rude. This would become a common thread with absolutely every person who had had any type of contact with James Massey.

True to form, the investigation moved forward. April 21 brought around a test of the mileage from Mom's house to the Albertsons', where Massey had rented a movie on the night of the murder. The goal, of course, was to see what kind of time it actually took to complete the round trip. Each road or highway taken by the investigator was listed in painstaking detail, with the miles listed to the tenth. Investigator McDaniel went as far as to mention his speeds. Bottom line total, start to finish, was five minutes and eleven seconds. Massey's version was that he had left the house, rented a movie at this location, and returned to find Mom in the bedroom. As we found out, within a few days of the murder, version two was the fight. Mom would have never gone into her bedroom and grabbed a gun. From the time I was little, I can still see her refusing to ever touch any type of firearm.

April 24, 1995, brought around our return trip to Duncanville, Texas. Jack, Susan, Sheri, and I didn't say a whole lot to one another on the way down. Stopping by the credit union, the City of Duncanville offices, plus the police station seemed to reopen my very deep emotional wounds. We had to make written statements with the detectives for evidence. Our feelings were that there would be no way Massey could get out of this. One key piece to the case was missing: the .22-caliber revolver. Plenty of ammunition for a gun like that had been found in his closet, but still no weapon had been discovered. The police had motive. It went without saying they had the body. Evidence was piling up by the boxfull. People kept coming forward with the same stories of Pat being scared of her husband; Massey showing up drunk in public making a fool of himself seemed to come up most often. His brash, abusive behavior toward Mom in public was mentioned in everyone's written statements. His part-time employer had even told the story of his waving a gun as he chased Mom throughout the house with threats of, "I'll kill you if you leave me" coming from his foul mouth.

Within my own statement, I noted that even before I met this clown he told me over the phone, "I'm marrying my retirement." I also included a letter I'd written Mom before I had met Massey face to face. Unlike Mom, I never dated anything back then. This was written around June of 1990.

Mom,

I've had a chance to think about what you have brought upon yourself and family. There's no other way but to be honest in this mess. I know what others think of your new found wonder boy really does matter to you. If he was the charming, 'Mr. Everything', you say or said he is or was, then I know I would have already met him. You want my opinion? No, I do not care for him. Twice, on the phone, I have hung up with bad vibes after talking to him. What John told me a week ago or so confirmed my feelings.

Who is this mouthy, big shot asshole who refers to ALL women as BITCHES?!! I think all women would include you, huh?

I feel left out here mom. Did you screw up? Hey, I'll gladly throw him out if you need it.

This guy is set in his ways. You're not going to mold him into anyone else. You act like you were looking for a fast ball and you got a curve. STRIKE!

Look at what you're doing and ask yourself:

1-What would my boss think?

2-What will the neighbors think? And of course,

3-What will Jack think?

Image has always been important to you. Now what kind are you creating for yourself?

No, I will not let you spend the night with him at my house.

No, I am no longer all for you getting married. Your judgment here has been blurred beyond recognition.

Don't ever tell me he reminds me of my dad. Dad never referred to you as a bitch.

Jim

Among the evidence, statements, photographs, and drawings was a list found after she had been shot. I am bewildered when I try to imagine her state of mind. The list, in her handwriting, reads like this:

1 bx. Bank Statements
1 bx Tax Returns
Insurance
Important Documents
CMA Statements in binders

Instructions for Survivors-
Name of Ins. Co.
Atty.
Funeral Arrangements
Location of Documents

Location of Bk. Accounts
Location of Outstanding Bills & due dates
Include, R.E. Taxes, etc.

We can only assume that the note below, dated 3/14/95, was her last to Massey. This may have been what fueled him to pull a gun and shoot my mother.

James
You know as very well as I do,
YOU HAVE A DRINKING PROBLEM.
You are not going to give your problem up for anyone.
Your liquor takes first priority in your life-
There is NO ROOM for a wife.
I can make it without you.
I wish you the very best loving your liquor.
Have a good drunken life.

For the next several months, various paperwork and reports flowed into the investigation. We had forensics, dozens of written statements, and countless hours of police work. Back at our house, we were surrounded with support. The Duncanville Police Department kept us informed on any updates to the case, which helped us deal with the situation. Making the trip to Duncanville became second nature for me. Jack and I now had a house to clean up. My brother's career would not allow him to take days off during the week. June of 1995 found me in-between jobs. With a little time on my hands, I made arrangements for a contractor to paint the inside of the house. Working with some nice folks in Duncanville, I found a flooring company that completely carpeted the home. Jack and I had taken a weekend to replace some privacy fence in back. All of the repairs were leading to the sale of the property.

Using Mom's attorney turned out to be another point of high stress. He told us both about a law in Texas. This law allowed for a surviving spouse to live in a dwelling that was shared with his or her husband or wife for as long as he or she chose. *No way* was that piece of flesh, James R. Massey, going to spend another minute in the house that my father had purchased for Mom. This law, according to lawyer Sam, prevented us from listing the house with a real estate agent. Fine. All we had was time, so this little bump in the road didn't upset me. Please understand that I was still responsible for closing out Mom's estate, finding a new profession, raising our family, and keeping my marriage intact. Once Sam started telling me he was on his way to the library to do research, I began doubting his ability. Telling me the first time was acceptable. I am pretty sure it was the third time he told me he was "just leaving for the library" when I exploded. With my vent stack shooting a mixture of flames and hot lava, I tore into this guy like a six-year-old opening a Christmas present. There was no question in Sam's mind that he no longer represented me or any member of my family, living or deceased. Within the week, the property located at 215 Hillcroft was listed for sale.

When Dad passed away in 1986 he had some life insurance. The agent wanted to sell Mom something, so he delayed delivering the proceeds. This act of unprofessional, disrespectful behavior prompted my entry into the life insurance business. I made myself the promise of always treating people the way I felt Mom should have been treated. In August of 1995 I had taken and passed all three required tests. The focus it took to accomplish all of the study prevented me from dwelling too deeply on the upcoming murder trial.

Chapter Eleven

The System

SEPTEMBER 19, 1995 WAS OUR first scheduled day in court. All of Mom's sisters had plane tickets ready to see that bastard hauled off to prison. Two weeks before the date, I called the district attorney.

"Sorry, Mr. Pulley, your scheduled court date has been postponed. No one told you?" What an unexpected response from the department representing our family.

"Postponed? What caused all of this?" My voice was frantic with disbelief.

"Court docket backed up with too many cases." This was their standard answer to an obvious question.

"When are we due back in court?" I asked quickly.

"January 22, 1996," came the cool, calm, collected voice on the other end.

Now I had to break this news to my family. Everyone was shocked. The wait was far from over. The whole unbelievable chain of events weighed heavily on my mind. Every situation seemed to be placing me front and center. I'm not certain where I was storing all of my frustrations, but I am sure it was not in a very healthy spot.

My office phone rang in October of 1995. The call was from a detective with the Irving, Texas, Police Department. His unit was looking for a truck involved in a hit and run. The front license plate had been knocked off of the pickup that did all of the damage. Low and behold the truck was registered in Mom's name. The cop told me he had been informed of Mother's death and passed along his condolences. He was calling me to find out if I had any idea of where Massey might be living. Knowing some of his past choices in lodging, I suggested that he start looking at all local hotels with a bar. No more than twenty minutes went by when, once again, the officer was calling. He was chuckling as he relayed the news of finding Massey at a local hotel. True to form, the hotel where the drunkard was staying had a bar. Case closed.

During this same period of time, the Community Supervision and Corrections Department for Dallas County sent this letter to James R. Massey.

Dear Mr. Massey,

Please be advised your request for unsupervised probation has been granted by the court. As of this date, you will no longer be required to report to a probation officer or pay any fees. However, if you have any new charges filed against you before your probation officially expires on 10/26/95, a warrant could be issued for your arrest and you may be required to appear before the judge.

Good luck in the future, if you have any questions, please feel free to call the undersigned officer.

Sincerely,

Ms. Potter

The "good luck" is what really catches your eye. Why wish a criminally disturbed individual any type of luck or good fortune?

Since we had not been kept informed of the original court date being cancelled, I decided to phone the DA's office in December. Once again the district attorney's office was sorry to inform me that the date had been backed up until April. Jack had heard enough. My brother shows brilliance at times. This had to be a banner moment. He insisted that we both go to the Frank Crowley Courts Buildings in Dallas to have a word with the people in charge of our case. We set an appointment with their office and took a day to travel. Trisha made the adult-like decision to accompany us on that day. Mom's case had been handed off to a young, fresh-faced assistant DA. Inside his office were four boxes of evidence. His confidence of getting a conviction was somewhere around 10 percent. The numbness we felt once he dropped this bombshell in our laps still resonates through my body.

"With all of the evidence you have collected, how can you not have a solid case?" I asked as I moved to the edge of my chair.

With his face reflecting the laser-like stares from the three of us, he nervously replied, "We can't put the gun in his possession."

As he went on to explain, most of the evidence was hearsay. The court considers this type of proof inadmissible. Massey's new lawyer had called the Duncanville Police in August to give them the location of the handgun. Six investigators loaded up their search team with the expectation of spending a day looking for the murder weapon. A metal detector found it within twenty minutes of their arrival. Lying in the side ditch, with part of the hand grip missing, and five live rounds in the chamber, was the little revolver used to shoot and kill Mom. James Massey had driven about a mile from the house, and tossed it out of the car. According to the DA, this key discovery had no impact on the case, since Massey's legal side had given it up. Now we had the gun, the body, the motive, and boxes full of hearsay evidence. The youngster in charge of our trial was now back-pedaling like a scared little boy.

We walked out of our meeting needing a stiff drink. The unthinkable was unfolding before our very eyes. How is it possible that a person can kill another in such an obvious fashion and walk away? No one thought he was innocent. Every written statement spoke of his violent, abusive behavior, plus threats on Mom's life. Mom's trust in telling so many people that he was threatening to kill her meant absolutely nothing. Now this case was strictly based on his word against a dead person's.

A solid year after her death, the court system was trying to convince us that the exhausting legwork performed by the detectives was all for naught. Late in March, I called to confirm our day of reckoning. For the third time, our day was delayed. Massey's attorney, Bubba, was running for judge. He found it necessary to put us off so he could shake hands and kiss babies. No problem, just another punch in the mouth from an overloaded legal system. After all, who are we to become upset?

Our court date was set for June 1996, with both sides having confirmed. After our conference with the DA's office, our family was ready to put closure on this unrealistic fog. For the fourth time, we were sent home. Bubba's father had presumably passed away. June would not be the month for our trial to begin.

Now came the final time for the Duncanville Police Department to call me in North Texas. They wanted to let me know of the new court date. July 15, 1996 was confirmed. Monday morning they would be selecting the jury. We were going to trial with the anticipation of watching the bum squirm. Visions of seeing this idiot for the first time in over two years bounced around my mind. Oh yes, we would all be in the front row. Close enough to hear the cuffs click as they led him off to the slammer!

The morning of the trial had a tremendously nervous tone about it. We had all assembled in the small office of our attorney. Final jury selection is like the NFL draft. Both sides go back and forth until all parties agree. For an unexplained reason, I felt a superhuman strength. The mind is a very powerful yet peculiar thing. Thoughts of getting both hands around his throat or kicking him until something in his body was broken had my adrenaline at a very high level. I now understand how a caged lion feels. Pacing the floor, with sweat dripping inside of my dress shirt, I had to get out of the office.

"I have to go to the restroom," I blurted out.

My wife looked at me funny and said, "You come right back."

Free from the confines of the small office, I set out to find the son-of-a-bitch who had shot my mom. I knew he had to be somewhere in the building. My fists were clenched as tight as my teeth. This no-good loud mouth had to be talking crap to someone. My mind raced with the anticipation of hearing his overbearing, cocky little voice. I was ready to move in and cause some serious pain.

On the main floor of the complex is where the court rooms are located. Outside of the rooms is a very large, window-encased waiting area. Glass double doors are the only way in or out. As I pushed the door open to enter the waiting area, I spotted what looked like his daughter, Jamie. Blood pressure of this proportion would knock most people out. My eyes started to hurt. Then, in an instant, my eyes focused on Massey. He was no more than six steps in front of me. His pace was quick as he literally walked right past me. Wheeling around, with no plan in mind, I stepped in right behind him. The fifteen months since Mom was killed had built up layers of hatred for this person. Every one of those bits and pieces of evil thoughts exploded in my body. He opened the door, turned right, and headed toward the men's room. Suddenly, everything in my line of site was blurred. I couldn't see anything but red, for about ten seconds. Stopping myself just outside of the glass double doors, I found a sheriff's deputy. With purpose, I made my way toward the officer.

"Don't let me leave this spot," I told him.

He looked at me as if to say, *What the heck is wrong with you?*

"There goes the guy who shot and killed my mom," was all my clouded mind could think to say.

I knew I had to get back upstairs to our meeting place. Standing beside the deputy seemed to bring me back to reality. Focusing on the elevators, I quickly made my way back upstairs. Sheri knew in an instant something was definitely wrong.

"Are you all right?" she exclaimed as she peered into my eyes.

"I saw him," came my empty reply.

"You stay here. Don't leave until they tell us to," my wife said in a firm but soothing manner.

From April of 1995 until July 1996 brought very significant changes to all of our lives. The moment arrived, and we were led to the court room. On the way down in the elevator, we stopped on the next floor below us. Bubba climbed into our car. Right beside me stood the person representing Massey. He had no clue who was a mere foot away.

Purposely turning to him I said, "Sorry to hear about your father."

He looked a little startled as he replied, "Thank you."

"I've lost both of my parents. My mother was shot and killed just last year," I said in a very controlled tone.

Once the door to the elevator opened, Bubba shot out of there like his shoes were burning.

As we moved toward the courtroom, I began to feel a peace coming over me. God was going to see to it that James R. Massey was convicted. My aunts had not made the trip. Shirley had spent so much money on ticket changes that she decided to excuse herself. Mom's other sisters usually do not fly, so they were not there, either. Any decisions made were going to come directly from me and my brother.

Before we ever got to the courtroom, we were stopped by the DA in the hallway. He asked us to return to the office upstairs, where he broke the news. Bubba had convinced Massey to plead guilty. Manslaughter will permanently remain on his record. We all looked at each other as if to say, "That's it?" The DA went on to explain that since jurors were selected from driver's license numbers, the pool of people would vary quite a bit.

"We could wind up with seven women-haters who could see things Massey's way," came one explanation from the DA.

"We could also have a jury made up of eight women who have been abused." The words coming from the assistant DA seemed to be telling us we could kick butt or get ours handed to us.

Jack and I excused ourselves. We met privately with our wives. The pressure of making the right call came down to Mom's only two children. We had been given the length of time Massey had agreed to: five years was it. I experienced dry mouth, sweating, confusion, uncertainty, crying, all of this in a very short time. If I swallowed once, I swallowed seventeen times. We were motivated by one thing: life-long regret if James R. Massey walked out of the courthouse a free man. Hanging our heads in semi-defeat, we agreed to the plea deal.

Making the arrangements was short and simple. All of us came into the court room. Massey's family did not acknowledge our glaring looks. His mommy and daughter were there. Knucklehead had already been led into the room and seated at the defendant's table directly in front of us.

The judge came in after the bailiff announced, "All rise." He read the agreement out loud. This was not his first rodeo. The look of disgust he was giving Massey told it all.

"How do you plead?" The judge was expecting the prearranged "guilty."

Right on cue, Massey spouts off, "Nolo Contendere." This response was *not* in the script.

This visibly upset the judge. "That is not an option!" The judge's response brought him to the edge of his high-backed leather chair.

Massey's ignorance had no boundaries. He finally said, "Guilty." The click of his handcuffs echoed through the room. He was walked out through a door reserved for those being carted off to jail.

Sighs of relief could be heard throughout our side. A few muffled whimpers came from across the aisle. I can still see them turning the other way as we all left. The two members of his family wouldn't even tell us, "Sorry for your loss." I wasn't expecting it, but they did know Mom.

Before leaving we found ourselves back in the office of the assistant DA. Detective Sims was there.

"Guys his age usually don't make it a year or two in the pen. He won't make it out alive." Alvin was very confident.

I thanked everyone for all the effort and time it took to make this happen. Down deep, neither Jack nor I could tell if what we had done was the right thing. We made the call to Mom's sisters to let them know it was finally over. As expected, they were all very disappointed in hearing the plea deal was only for five years. I am sure they second-guessed us for going in that direction instead of insisting on a full trial. Watching him walk out as he waved to us would have taken twenty years off our lives.

Chapter Twelve

Forgiveness

It was late in the day, so we decided to stay the night. The morning came around quickly.

Knowing exactly what I had to do, I showered, put on my best suit, and left the room.

Holding my head up high, I drove to Little Bethel Cemetery in Duncanville, Texas.

Under the shade of oak trees lay a couple of good people. We had a nice conversation that morning. In honor of my dad I wore a red, white, and blue tie. My suit was black.

We were all in mourning for the horrific way Mom had been taken from us.

When all was said and done, a memorial book collection was established at the Duncanville Public Library, where Carla Bryan is director. She knew Mom personally, so the motivation for making the collection work has been easy for her. Carla sets all of the books in the collection out during the week of Mom's birthday, March 17. The books stay checked out, so in some way, we are trying to give back. Most of the books deal with elevating self-esteem. Some are written on the subject of living with an alcoholic, and a few take on the subject of abuse.

Having never gone through anything as unspeakable as the murder of a parent, none of us knew how to deal with its aftermath. My answer was to focus on my career. Meeting new people was fun and never boring. I found myself bringing up the past. Talking to others about our experience seemed like the right thing to do. It soon became evident that we were not alone. Many individuals and families suffer unexpected losses. Pain is not a welcome sensation, but sharing, however awkward, can be somewhat therapeutic. Emptiness ran deep through my soul. Anger at what had taken place burned inside like a small flame. I would flare up in an instant with emotional outbursts. My personal behavior had been altered. I had no way of understanding what it would take to relieve my mind of the tension and frustration left from the events that had transpired.

I am always looking for the next best thing, whatever is best for my family, business, or personal growth. God's word has been instrumental in my progress toward forgiveness. Purely letting go of hatred toward another isn't something I've ever dwelled on. During the course of our lives, situations change. Deep within us all, the events of our past can still dictate our thoughts and feelings. My first reaction to the person who pleaded guilty to Mom's murder was to see him fry in the electric chair. I often contemplate the idea of someone dying at the hands of another. Sadly, we see it every day in the world.

I know it is impossible to share emotions and reactions with someone else. No one can fully recreate what I felt on the day I got the news of

Mom's killing. The pressure of making the decision of whether to take this case to a jury trial weighed heavily on both my brother and me. Jack and I were geared up for a lengthy trial. That swelling went away in a moment once Massey agreed to his plea deal. The day of the trial went from 110 mph to a dead halt in a flash. Internally I went from heavy breathing to breathless. There is only one person to point to when I think of the cause. My disgust at the thought of James Massey being in our family can bring me to anger and rage if I allow it.

Forgiving him for his abuse, controlling actions, disrespectful behavior, and the taking of Mom's life is impossible. Asking God to forgive me for wishing him dead is acceptable. I have asked for divine guidance in shaping my future. Psalms 1:1-3 from the *Living Bible* says: "Oh, the joys of those who do not follow evil men's advice, who do not hang around with sinners, scoffing at the things of God: But they delight in doing everything God wants them to, and day and night are always meditating on his laws and thinking about ways to follow him more closely. They are like trees along a river bank bearing luscious fruit each season without fail. Their leaves shall never wither, and all they do shall prosper." Romans 3:10-18 says: "No one is good—no one in all the world is innocent. No one has ever really followed God's paths, or even truly wanted to. Everyone has turned away; all have gone wrong. No one anywhere has kept on doing what is right; not one. Their talk is foul and filthy like the stench from an open grave. Their tongues are loaded with lies. Everything they say has in it the sting and poison of deadly snakes. Their mouths are full of cursing and bitterness. They are quick to kill, hating anyone who disagrees with them. Wherever they go they leave misery and trouble behind them, and they have never known what it is to feel secure or enjoy God's blessing. They care nothing about God nor what He thinks of them."

What this is telling us is that we are all wired to fail. Without guidance from above, and God's hands on the reins, our personal lives would run wild.

Taking baby steps in the direction of my beliefs has been a positive pace in my effort to forgive. God knows what horrible acts were done on the night the hammer was pulled back on the little Saturday night special, aimed at Mom's face, and the trigger pulled. Cold and callous, my mother's husband left her to die on the bedroom floor. He blamed an outside intruder and even tried to point the finger at Mom. Forgive him? How? No, sir. I can only ask God to let me live as normal a life as any man. Let my thoughts of violent retaliation go. Please take away the nightmares, the grinding of my teeth, and the distractions caused by this depressing family tragedy.

I feel I have a long way to go: Matthew 6:14-15 from the *Living Bible* says: "Your heavenly Father will forgive you if you forgive those who sin against you; but if you refuse to forgive them, he will not forgive you." Mark 11:25 says: "But when you are praying, first forgive anyone you are holding a grudge against, so that your Father in Heaven will forgive you and your sins too." Lastly, Luke 6: 36-37 says: "Try to show as much compassion as your Father does. Never criticize or condemn—or it will all come back on you. Go easy on others; then they will do the same for you."

I can only ask God to forgive James Massey of the sin against Mom. I need to find a way to ask Him to forgive me of my thoughts toward Massey.

My own healing comes and goes. Trauma can cause unknown changes to one's own personality. My profession places me in front of several quality individuals. I was asked to speak at a gathering for First Step, an organization designed to assist those caught in the hell of family violence.

I had my speech ready. Our daughter Trisha came along to support me. Everything was fine until I stood up to approach the podium. Those eleven years of suppressed feelings opened up the floodgates. The easiest way out was through my tear ducts. Delivering a speech while choked up is next to impossible. All forms of media were on hand to record my very public emotional meltdown. The story of Mom's murder was printed, along with a picture of me drowning in tears. I have since spoken about the experience without blowing a gasket. Sharing seems to be an effective way of dealing with so many feelings. Willingly, I offer this true account to the world. I realize there have been many other families affected by the senseless acts of others. The chain reaction of pain can be felt throughout an entire family.

It's rare that you ever know the impression you leave on others. It is with heartfelt sincerity that I hope this book has left a positive and motivational impression on you.

Epilogue

Resources

Please visit our website; www.patcanhelp.com. We have listed several resources for those in need of assistance.

As I mentioned, there is a collection of books in Mom's name. Patricia L. Pulley has over thirty books in the Duncanville library. All of the publications can be viewed at the library's website: www.youseemore. com/duncanville.

My brother and I wanted to give back to those in need. The director, Carla Bryan, always has her eyes open for literature that touches on the subject or related areas of family violence.

There are several good reads offering assistance at different levels. A friend of mine, Diane Cunningham, suggested the Boundaries series by author Henry Cloud.

Patricia Evans has written two books: *Verbally Abusive Relationship*, and *Controlling People*.

I completely understand that some people do not care to read. I also know that people in a true crisis situation may not have the time. The United Way has created a system that is available in 80 percent of the U.S. 2-1-1 is an easy number to remember and dial. The operators have a database of resources right in front of them. This crisis call center is designed to offer suggestions for a variety of individuals. They can help with child care, housing, education, employment, counseling, even suicide. They take calls 24/7.

Locally, First Step is an organization that serves an eleven-county area. Their services are many. Your community may not be as fortunate as some. If that is the case, there is a number to the National Domestic Violence Hot Line: 800-799-SAFE.

I visited with the education coordinator at First Step here in Wichita Falls, Texas. She enlightened me about some of the procedures currently in place. One in particular was the fact that a big percentage of youthful runaways come from abusive homes. If you know anyone in this situation, there are seven toll-free numbers to contact. The numbers listed are national:

Childhelp USA
1-800-422-4453
24/7 hotline

Child Find of America
1-800-426-56789
Mon-Fri 9 a.m. to 5 p.m.

Covenant House Hotline
Runaway youth
1-800-999-9999
24-hour hotline

Child Quest International Sighting
1-888-818-4673

National Center for Missing and Exploited Children
1-800-843-5678

Rape Abuse and Incest National Network (RAINN)
1-800-656-4673

USA National Suicide Hotlines
Teen Suicide
1-800-784-2433

There is one other group I would like to mention. In Austin, Texas, there is the Texas Council on Family Violence. They can be reached at: 512-794-1133

Whether you are in Texas or any other state, the above-listed resources could have a positive impact on you or a loved one. Do not hesitate to contact them if you feel one or more can help.

Most churches can offer some sort of counseling. Don't leave your religious beliefs out of a life-altering decision. My God has been helpful.